GOPHER GOLD

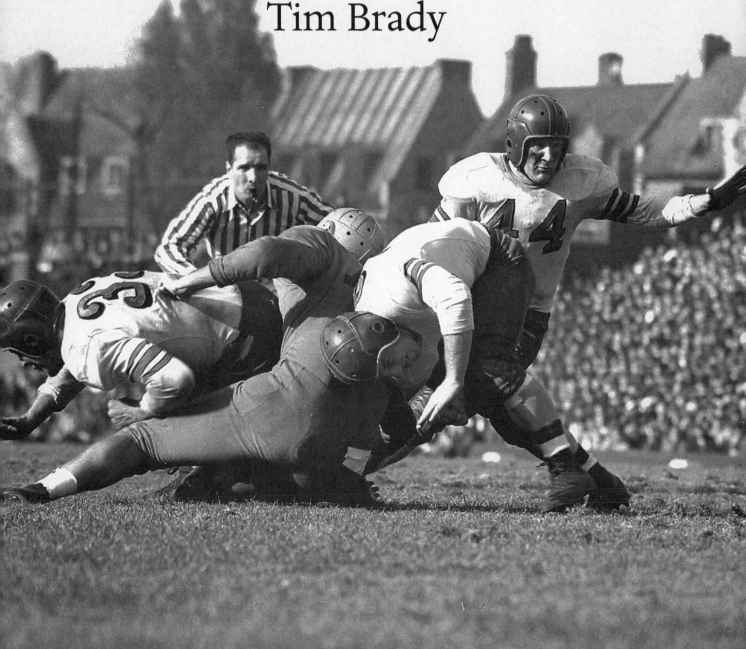

GOPHER GOLD

Legendary Figures, Brilliant Blunders,
and Amazing Feats at the University of Minnesota

Tim Brady

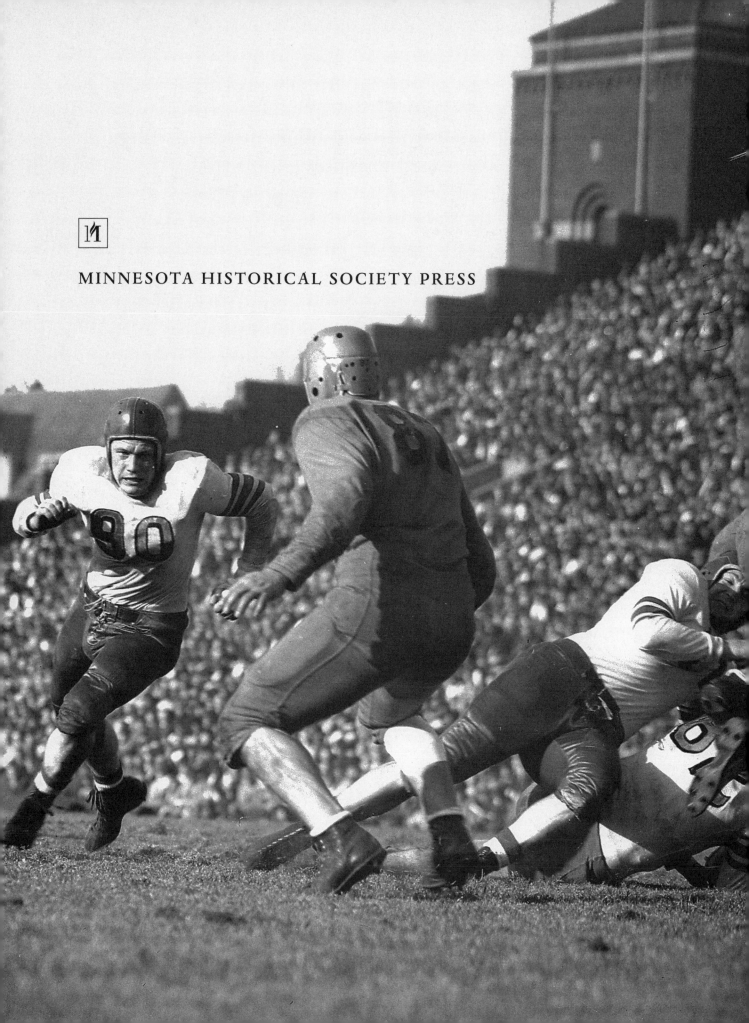

MINNESOTA HISTORICAL SOCIETY PRESS

Earlier versions of the following pieces were first published in
these magazines: "King Red" and "A Spectacular Career"
in *Minnesota Monthly;* "Farsighted Foresters" in *Minnesota Conservation
Volunteer;* all others in *Minnesota Magazine.*

www.mhspress.org

The Minnesota Historical Society Press is a member of
the Association of American University Presses.

Manufactured in the United States of America

10 9 8 7 6 5 4 3 2 1

♾ The paper used in this publication meets the minimum requirements of
the American National Standard for Information Sciences—Permanence for
Printed Library Materials, ANSI Z39.48-1984.

International Standard Book Number
ISBN 13: 978-0-87351-601-3 (cloth)
ISBN 10: 0-87351-601-X (cloth)

Title-page photo: University of Minnesota Gophers versus Ohio State, 1945

Library of Congress Cataloging-in-Publication Data

Brady, Tim, 1955–
    Gopher gold : legendary figures, brilliant blunders, and amazing feats at the
University of Minnesota / Tim Brady.
        p. cm.
Includes bibliographical references.
ISBN-13: 978-0-87351-601-3 (cloth : alk. paper)
ISBN-10: 0-87351-601-X (cloth : alk. paper)
1. University of Minnesota—History. I. Title.
LD3348.B73 2007
378.776′579—dc22
                                                                2007017311

To Wallace and Mary Brady

Contents

Preface

THE UNIVERSITY OF MINNESOTA has brought a wealth of talent and ability to Minnesota and the surrounding region—and given just as much to the wide world beyond. The university is one of the country's great land grant institutions, and the value that these schools bring to the various regions they serve is too often forgotten or too readily accepted. It is a cliché to say that the University of Minnesota is a treasure to the state, yet that remains a basic truth. All of us who live in Minnesota are made richer by its existence.

Gopher Gold: Legendary Figures, Brilliant Blunders, and Amazing Feats at the University of Minnesota is a collection of history stories that suggest some of this lasting value and achievement. These pieces, written primarily for *Minnesota*, the alumni magazine of the University of Minnesota, also give a flavor of how lives were led at the university from its earliest days forward.

Many people have had a hand in the creation of these stories, but no one has been more essential to their existence than Shelly Fling, editor of *Minnesota Magazine*. Shelly not only edited all of the pieces that first appeared in the alumni magazine but also suggested many of the topics and has been a smart and scrupulous adviser in their creation. It has been a rare pleasure working with her, and I wish all writers such good luck in their relationships with their editors.

I'd also like to thank Margaret Sughrue Carlson, executive director of the University of Minnesota Alumni Association, whose appreciation for the university's history has made her a faithful fan and advocate for these stories.

At the University of Minnesota Archives, Lois Hendrickson and Karen Klinkenberg have been incredibly supportive and helpful in finding the essential documents that form the basis of many of these pieces.

At the Minnesota Historical Society Press, Ann Regan, editor in chief, has been a terrific help in organizing these stories, turning them into an accessible collection and guiding the book toward publication. Ann has offered unerringly good counsel from the moment she laid eyes on them. Thanks also to editor Marilyn Ziebarth for her good work collecting the images and to Dorothea Anderson for her fine copyediting work.

I'd also like to thank Jeff Johnson and Joel Hoekstra, editors at *Minnesota Monthly*, where "King Red" and "A Spectacular Career" first appeared, in slightly altered forms; and Kathleen Weflen, editor of *Minnesota Conservation Volunteer*, where "Farsighted Foresters" was first published, also in a slightly altered version.

Finally, I thank Susan, who has always been my best and most faithful reader, and Hannah and Sam, just for being who they are.

Campus Life

The first president
of the university,
William Watts Folwell,
about 1888

A. G. BUSHNELL, NEW YORK.

Very truly yours,
William W. Folwell.

Guns and Scholars

I N THE WEE HOURS of the morning on May 16, 1882, a group of University of Minnesota debate students and their fans, a little jiggy from having just suffered an upset defeat at the hands of the Clayonian Club of St. Paul, decided to vent their frustrations at the home of William Watts Folwell, president of the university. The plan was to hijack the front gates leading up to Folwell's house and . . . do something with them. Precisely what was never ascertained. This was to be a symbolic gesture more than anything else, an act of defiance meant to suggest that the president ought to open the doors of the campus to a little more personal freedom. Cut these students some slack.

It wasn't the first time that Folwell had been chosen as the target of pent-up student emotions. Several months prior to this May evening, to protest a demerit system imposed by Folwell, a group of university students had kidnapped the president's horse — a high crime in 1882. They clipped the poor animal's tail and mane and wrapped its hooves in burlap sacks to quiet a trip up to the tower of Old Main, the central and nearly only structure standing on the campus at the time. Again history fails to say exactly what the students were going to do with the horse once they got him up there. At any rate, they were apprehended in the midst of the act, and the protest of the demerit system prompted Folwell to use it once again.

Rambunctious students weren't Folwell's only problem in the spring of 1882. Hired in 1869 as the first president of the University of Minnesota, Folwell was a visionary educator, a man in the forefront of the college reform movement that swept the nation in the second half of the nineteenth century. In a speech given to the state legislature soon after he was hired, Folwell outlined an ambitious plan for the university, which anticipated the school's twentieth-century status in the state. The university would not only serve

The University of Minnesota, Minneapolis, Minn.

A few buildings and spacious grounds marked the university's campus, early 1880s.

as the higher education center of a statewide system of education; it would also be a resource for the entire population, providing know-how to business and government and feeding talent to the arts and science communities.

Trouble was, when Folwell gave this speech, the University of Minnesota campus consisted of Old Main, a bare-bones budget, and a penny-pinching regent's board. Folwell had no staff beyond the faculty and served as college president, secretary, librarian, and chief janitor. The faculty itself was a hide-bound lot dominated by a group of ministers more interested in drumming the classics into their scholars than in any grand vision of what the college could be. And the student body was a quintessentially nineteenth-century mix of would-be Victorian gentlemen and -women and young frontier yahoos.

By 1882, Folwell had brought in a largely new faculty, including the redoubtable Maria Sanford. He also helped get the moribund college of agriculture off the ground. But at the same time, the university wasn't growing. There were fewer students enrolled in 1882 than there had been a dozen years earlier, and for both Folwell and the regents, the bloom was off the rose. Word was that he was not quite the stout fellow needed to build the grand state university of his own envisioning.

On the night of the debate (the question of the evening: "Resolved, that the United States should have Tariff for Revenue only"), William Folwell was clearly in no mood to see his gates ripped off by a gang of rowdy students. Somehow he got wind of their plans, and he called a couple of faculty members over to his house to stand guard with him and foil the plot. The professors were John G. "Dutchy" Moore, a teacher of German, and W. A. Pike, the sole member of the Engineering Department at the university. Pike, an MIT grad and recent addition to the faculty, made the mistake of sticking a pistol in his pocket before heading to his lookout in Folwell's parlor.

Young university students clowning for the camera, 1900s

Across campus, his head full of the wrongs of both Folwell's demerit system and the U.S. tariff, Asa Paine, the sophomore son of a piney woods lumberman from northern Minnesota, came galumphing toward destiny.

He, too, was packing heat.

In measuring the long heartbeat of the University of Minnesota, what happened next would, in time, appear to be just an excited blip on the monitor. But few anecdotes serve as a better indicator of just how far the college has come since its beginnings in the middle of the nineteenth century.

To picture a university president and esteemed members of his faculty brawling in the dark with a group of students, the two groups pulling guns on each other, suggests a wilder day and age. And it's true that Minnesota, in 1882, was a volatile place. Hordes of immigrants and newcomers were streaming through the Twin Cities on their way to the wheat fields of the Dakotas and the western portions of Minnesota. The populations of Minneapolis and St. Paul were likewise exploding, and the mills of Minneapolis were starting to grind so much wheat into flour that they might as well have been minting money.

The front pages of the St. Paul papers were periodically filled with promotions for would-be towns to the west: Endless land! The railroad's a-coming! Winters: Not so bad! But inside the paper, the news was often darker. Local police departments were being asked to round up "bummers" hanging out by the railroad yards. In the same month as the incident at Folwell's gate, a "tramp" was accused of "outraging" a little girl in Le Sueur, and the story of the ensuing manhunt filled columns for days. A recent lynching of a man referred to in the paper simply as "the rogue McManus" served as backdrop to the search and ominous warning to the fugitive if he were ever caught.

The air of frontier violence might have wafted over the campus, but, by itself, it can't quite explain the free-for-all that ensued.

It was two o'clock in the morning. From their vantage point at Folwell's house at 1020 Fifth Street Southeast, the professors and the president saw the gang of students in front of his home. Somehow they had already swiped the gates and were making off with them when Folwell and company gave chase. According to an account two days later in the *New York Times*, Folwell pursued the main body of boys, while Moore and Pike lit out after Asa Paine. As Paine raced away, Pike pulled out his 22-caliber pistol and hollered something like, "Halt! You gate thief!" This, according to the *Times*, "invited [Paine] to greater speed."

Moore soon caught up with the boy and started thrashing him with a cane until Paine was finally knocked to the ground in front of Professor

Pike's residence, just down the street from Folwell's home. It was at this point that Paine pulled out his own revolver from beneath his coat and leveled it at Moore. According to the *Times*, he said, "I can't stand this; stop or I will shoot!"

Now W. A. Pike arrived with his own pistol drawn. Seeing his colleague with a gun pointed at his midsection and assuming that the German Department was about to have a huge hole in it, W. A. Pike plugged Asa Paine in the leg. "I am shot," the young man said with simple drama. He was hauled back to Folwell's house, where a doctor was called to tend to his wound. It would turn out to be minor. In fact, he probably felt no greater pain than President William Folwell and his two faculty members as they stood, the next day, arraigned in the docket of a Minneapolis courtroom, charged with assault and battery against one of their own students.

The May 18 *Minneapolis Evening Journal* gives a sense of the ignominy: "Yesterday morning after the usual grist of plain drunks and vagrants had been disposed of in the municipal court the names of W. W. Folwell, W. A. Pike and J. G. Moore were called by the clerk."

* * *

The university's faculty in 1890 included William Watts Folwell, John G. Moore, Cyrus Northrop, and George E. MacLean (seated, second, fourth, fifth, and ninth from left); Maria Sanford (second row, second from left); and William A. Pike (third row, far left).

W. A. PIKE WAS hardly a wild hare. He would, in the end, serve for more than twenty years with distinction at the University of Minnesota, founding the College of Mechanic Arts and serving as its first dean. W. W. Folwell was one of the most cultivated men in Minnesota, "interested in everything from Plato to hog cholera," according to one colleague. He was on a first-name basis with some of the leading academic and cultural figures of the day, including Charles Eliot, esteemed president of Yale University, and the renowned cultural critic Matthew Arnold. At a later time, he would write the first comprehensive history of the state of Minnesota and serve, after his presidency, for over forty years as a professor of political science on the university faculty.

And the students weren't exactly Billy the Kids. Days after the event, the student journal, the *Ariel*, took pains to defend the student body against charges of hooliganism: "We feel justified in declaring that in respect to scholarly deportment and high-minded, manly character, the students of this institution are not excelled by any other student body in the land. It is not true that we have among us an excepted few who are specimens of depravity, or sheep of a very dark color."

None of which mattered much to local public opinion. The *Minneapolis Evening Journal* suggested that the culprits might be better served by "an education in the penitentiary at Stillwater instead of the State University." "Folwell must go!" screamed the *St. Paul Pioneer Dispatch* in a column that mixed pithy editorial comments and tidbits of news from around the country: "Minnesota should change her University, so-called, into a school of gunnery." "The State University, so-called, should engage a professor of rifle practice." Et al.

For all of the sound and fury, there was a curious lack of sustained outrage at the incident. The general criticism leveled at Folwell and company had more to do with their inability to maintain discipline than the fact that they wound up trying to restore it with canes and guns. And as for the students—a kind of boys-will-be-boys defense was offered by the *Ariel*, which wrote: "It is a sorrowful fact that many educational institutions are unfortunate enough to number among their members some persons who continually engage in disgraceful proceedings from a pure love of deviltry." Never mind that there is deviltry, and deviltry with a pistol in your pocket. Guns, as we all know, were often brandished on the frontier.

During the campus shenanigans, few if any observers questioned the sort of paternalism cloaking the student body at Minnesota, as elsewhere across the country, that might have made any testosterone-driven young thing a little crazy. College students were generally considered as existing in that netherworld between child- and adulthood and were treated with a firm and guiding hand that was often rebelled against. The University of Minnesota was not the only American campus to experience an occasional outbreak of violence in the nineteenth century. In Madison, at the University of Wisconsin, brawls between "townies" and "gownies" were frequent, as was internecine warfare among students in various colleges at the university, such as law and engineering. The occasional riot, or "rush," was seen all over the nation. One of the reasons for the advent and popularity of intercollegiate sports like football in the late nineteenth century was to channel student aggression into constructive mayhem.

Like virtually all academic administrators in his day, Folwell ran a tight ship. Every morning at 8:30 sharp, students were expected to be in chapel, no ifs, ands, or buts about it. No alcohol, no tobacco, no gambling anywhere on campus. Classes were crammed into five periods in the forenoon, and the rest of the day students were expected to study and work. Folwell frowned on fraternities, and the only dorm rooms were found in the all-purpose Old Main. Even these were confiscated after 1870 to make room for more classes. The student body of 1882 consisted of a little over two hundred young men and women, ranging in age from their mid-teens to their mid-twenties. Because there were so few secondary schools in the state (the city of Minneapolis had built its first high school, Central High, in 1873), the university served the dual function of prepping students for higher education and then giving them one. Students typically spent about six years on campus getting their degrees.

Tuition was free, but most students had to work long hours to pay their living expenses. Books for a year of study cost about $15. Weekly expenses were in the neighborhood of five bucks, including room and board at one of the various boardinghouses in the area near campus that catered to a student clientele. The university offered the following advice to incoming students, to help alleviate economic problems:

1. If possible learn a good trade before coming to the University.
2. Bring some money, $50.00 at least, on which to live until you find work.
3. If you want to work, you must look for it. It will not come to you at first. Be active, resolute, and enterprising.
4. If you have to pay your way through college, resolve to take enough time to do it without ruining your health.

No mention was made of having your health ruined by a faculty member. Not that Asa Paine's wound was debilitating. In fact, it was healed in a matter of days—a thing that helped calm frayed nerves on campus. Still, the student body was up in arms enough to vote, by a wide majority a few

days after the incident, that Folwell tender his resignation. He didn't, and the Board of Regents failed to ask for it. But as indicated by the *New York Times*'s interest ("The Extraordinary Shooting Affray at the Minnesota State University" was the subhead of its May 18 front-page story), the embarrassing tale was picked up by newspapers elsewhere in the nation. Locally, sentiment remained strongly skeptical about Folwell's abilities to run the university. His many friends in the academic community both in Minnesota and across the country, however, rallied to his support and sent endorsements that helped save his job.

In the immediate aftermath of the shooting, Folwell pled guilty to technical assault, but no punishment was assessed by the court.

John G. "Dutchy" Moore also pled guilty to the charges of assault and was fined $25.

W. A. Pike's case was bound over to a grand jury, which in the fall of 1882 found no bill of indictment against him. Although his legal trials were over, Pike's health was apparently strained by the ordeal, and, according to the

Ariel, he took a leave of absence from the university that fall and "is currently at the seashore." He returned the next term.

There is no record of Asa Paine ever graduating from the university. In the same issue in which it records Pike's leave, the *Ariel* provides a rather glib coda to the shooting victim's collegiate career: "Asa Paine, '84, who was wounded in the famous 'Schutzenfest' last spring[,] is at the Northern Pacific Junction and probably will not return to school."

Folwell's tenure as president lasted two more years, but he lived for another fifty, all of which he spent on or near the University of Minnesota campus. He was able to see his dream of a statewide educational system headed by an esteemed university come to life. Perhaps, too, he lived long enough to forget the days of Old Main and chasing gate-snatching students in the middle of the night.

Professor Moore,
fined $25 for thrashing
a student with a cane

Company Q, the popular women's drill team that sparked the creation of a physical education program, 1889

The Broom Brigade

O N THE DAY IT REOPENED after the Civil War, in 1867, the University of Minnesota became the third state college to admit women. The sexes shared classrooms and college experiences, but they also maintained separate spheres dictated by gender and the Victorian mores of the time. Men at the university could play football, join the debate club, and enjoy the liberties of youth; women were given "a room of their own," in the form of a ladies' lounge in Old Main, that was strictly off-limits to men.

Most at the university were proud of its coeducation and felt it signified a progressive, "Western" view of higher education. One of the eleven women in the 1888 class of thirty-five graduates was Ima Winchell. In an essay in the *Ariel*, she wrote: "What a revolution! The opening of the higher institutions of learning to women has marked an era in history. Young women began to desire a college education and to appreciate the powers that they possessed, only needing development in order to place them where they could do their part in the world's work. This higher education spread before women many fields of work, and opened to her pursuits hitherto unknown."

Of course, not all fields were open to women in the Victorian era. In fact, just a few months after Ima Winchell's graduation, the women of the university would band together and knock firmly on a door that had been closed to them since the school's inception. What followed brought no earth-shattering change to the University of Minnesota, but it was probably the first collective action by female students of the U and turned out to be the crucial link in a chain that would lead all the way to the present.

A brief note tucked in with some other campus announcements in the back pages of the October 31, 1888, *Ariel* signaled the coming turn of events: "Lieutenant Edwin Glenn has a battalion of about one hundred and seventy-

five volunteers, whom he instructs in military science and tactics every day in the Coliseum," it read. "The ladies of the University have also petitioned for military drill, which will be granted them as soon as the necessary arrangements can be made."

It may seem odd that the Victorian-era women of the University of Minnesota would be eager to tote rifles and promenade, but this request for equal opportunity made perfect sense to the women of the class of '89. Military drill was a popular form of exercise in the post–Civil War era, and judged drill competitions between rival college battalions were a familiar entertainment. It wasn't the chance to play with guns that inspired the coeds as much as the opportunity to move their feet and stretch their muscles.

Gratia Countryman, who would later become a guiding force in the Minneapolis Public Library system, was one of Lieutenant Glenn's petitioners. Years after the events, she would recall the genesis of the women's drill squad:

"As I remember, the girls of my day had no provision for physical development or exercise. The boys had football and baseball. They had bicycles long before there were any provided for women. I cannot recall that there were tennis courts or any provision for anything in which women could participate. So when Lieutenant Glenn was engaged to give military drill to the boys, the girls felt that we deserved some attention, too."

A lot of "girls" felt they deserved the attention. Countryman hints that because the faculty, which received the petition, and Glenn, who would be instructing, were doubtful about the seriousness of the women on campus, they were quick to grant permission.

First Lieutenant Gratia Countryman, Company Q, who later became the guiding force behind the Minneapolis Public Library system

But the coeds came out in droves, and before the university knew what had hit it, there was a company of women doing military drill on campus. They quickly designed a uniform and gave themselves a name: Company Q. The Q, according to some, stood for "queens," though company members never revealed its precise meaning to the public.

Meanwhile, campus "kings" were left a little open-mouthed by all of this. The all-male staff of the *Ariel* gave a tongue-in-cheek description of Company Q's first meeting: "One morning near the close of the fall term the young ladies were made happy by the announcement that Lieutenant Glenn would be in the parlor after chapel to meet those of them who wished to receive military instruction. The girls flew down stairs, increasing the cadence to two hundred and forty steps a minute, and before the Lieutenant could enunciate a preparatory command he was surrounded by about a hundred raw recruits, all doing their best to throw him into confusion."

Actually, the number of women who signed up for the company was closer to fifty, including elected officers: Captain Ada Smith, First Lieutenant Gratia Countryman, Second Lieutenant Louise Montgomery, and First Sergeant Clara Baldwin. Their uniforms were made of the same gray-blue broadcloth as the men's uniforms. Black stripes lined the floor-length skirts and crisscrossed the blouses. Wooden guns were issued instead of the real things, but, according to Countryman, they "served perfectly well."

Two squads were formed, and the women drilled daily through the winter months of 1888–89 behind closed doors in the Coliseum. They used their wooden guns to practice the manual of arms and learned a standard set of drills and marches that included step, double step, common time, quick time, back and side steps, and marching in line and column and by the flank and to the rear. They learned to oblique, turn, and wheel, on both fixed and moveable points. They also did "sundry calisthenics and other gymnastics," according to Countryman.

Maybe it was the closed doors of the Coliseum; maybe it was the mystery of the company's name or the general secretiveness of its operations; maybe it was the "sub-bass war-whoops" passersby heard coming from inside; but a certain mystique gathered around the women who were drilling, evident in a march-step poem that eventually appeared in the pages of the *Ariel*:

> Q? Q? Q? Q?
> What is Company "Q"?
> A troop of girls,
> A troop well known as the pride of the U,
> A troop deserving of homage, too
> Maids who dress in black and blue,
> Maids whose cheeks are ruddy in hue,
> Maids who are blithe and bonny and true—
> Such a troop is Company "Q."

Word of these happenings spread beyond the campus, but not everyone who heard the legend of Company Q was as charmed as the poet. A *Minneapolis Tribune* editorial of December 4, 1888, was brutal in its assessment: The girls should be taught to dust, scrub, sew, build kitchen fires, and perform other domestic feats, instead of being initiated into the mysteries of military tactics: "Instead of guns, take brooms; teach girls to give a light, quick, short stroke, that sends dust ahead, and not to flirt it into the air and over the furniture with long, heavy swathes, as most women do." Back on campus, the editors at the *Ariel* took a more sophisticated stance on the matter—and dipped it in sarcasm:

> In spite of all statements to the contrary, and in spite of the fact that the women of our day practice law and medicine, edit newspapers, engage in politics and even teach school, we assert that the equality of the sexes is far from established, even in the advanced civilization which is supposed to permeate the University. If it were, we should not have to record the unjust discrimination which was exercised against the ladies in the matter of military instruction. Of course the ladies are entitled to the advantages of military drill and we are glad that they have made known their wishes to the faculty. A "broom brigade" will doubtless add materially to the value of the University as an educational center.

A hard-won women's physical education class, 1904

The "broom brigade" made its first public appearance in March 1889 for a photo-taking session for the *Gopher* yearbook. The *Ariel*, which kept up the snickering, was quick to note the wooden guns and the fact that the officers of Company Q had to borrow swords for the occasion. It also described a crowd that was disappointed with the fact that Q did not perform an exhibition drill after its photo session.

Those clamoring to see the women in action had to wait until commencement week for the opportunity, but they would not be disappointed. Before a large Saturday night crowd gathered for a pregraduation ceremony and ball at the coliseum, the women of Company Q took the floor. They proceeded to go through their setting-up exercises, the manual of arms, and their numerous marching movements "with scarcely a break." By the time they had finished, the audience was on its feet, whooping.

"We were never accused of complimenting the ladies, or repeating to them those of others, but the truth must be told," wrote the editors of the *Ariel*. "Company Q has been a brilliant success." So brilliant, in fact, that by the start of the next school year the university had decided to make drill a requirement for freshmen coeds. There were now so many young women under Glenn's command that he was forced to create a second company, which was dubbed "Q-Prime."

Gratia Countryman remained a loyal soldier through the next year, her last at the university. She recalled the growing expertise of Q in her reminiscence of the company: "The second year, Miss Baldwin was Captain and a splendid one. We were giving an exhibition with the galleries packed. The Company was marching in fours and seemed to be marching straight into a wall, from which we saw no escape, when she suddenly gave an order to wheel, and we made a beautiful turn with less than a yard to spare. We were greeted with explosions of applause."

Company Q remained a campus institution for just three more years. In the summer of 1892, the University of Minnesota hired Louise Kiehle to head a newly created Department of Physical Culture for women on campus, obviating the need for the exercise that came with military drill. A more conventional regimen of physical fitness was established for coeds, including a tennis program, calisthenics, and, by 1897, basketball.

Today the wooden guns and the blue-and-black broadcloth uniforms are ancient history. Long gone is Q. But echoes of the 1889 whoops can still be heard after every display of women's athleticism, from a free throw in the humblest of intramural games to a driving layup by a Golden Gopher star at Williams Arena.

Trailblazers and Jim Crow

IN MAY 1882, the University of Minnesota graduated its first African American student, Andrew Hilyer, who was one of only 34 seniors. Some 180 others attended college on a campus that consisted of exactly two buildings. Students rubbed elbows every day in chapel, in classes, and while doing chores like stoking the furnace of Old Main. According to *Recollections of Early University Days* (1934) by Hilyer's classmate Elmer Ellsworth Adams, "During the time that [Hilyer] was in college there was never any discrimination against him on account of his color, but he mingled with his classmates on almost perfect equality. [Hilyer] was intelligent in every way, a good scholar, [who made] quite a reputation [on campus] as an orator."

It may be presumptuous for a white student to write that there was never any discrimination against Andrew Hilyer, but there are hints that the University of Minnesota was a more collegial place for African American students in Hilyer's time than it would be by the 1920s and 1930s. Professional schools, particularly the Law School, the School of Pharmacy, and the School of Dentistry, were open to black students, and quite a few undergraduates, including women, attended and graduated from the university.

Many of these would join a small but growing professional class of black Minnesotans, most of whom lived in the Twin Cities. It was a community with some national distinctions. In St. Paul at the turn of the century, a larger percentage of African Americans owned their own homes than was the case in any other city in the United States. Black Minnesotans had comparatively lower rates of illiteracy than African Americans in any other region in the nation, just 3.4 percent. A thriving black press and a burgeoning number of African American community lodges, societies, leagues, and protective associations encouraged and promoted educational advancement within the community.

Student Gale Hilyer, the son of Andrew Hilyer, who was the university's first African American graduate, in 1882 (*1914* Gopher *annual*)

Andrew Hilyer moved to Washington, D.C., soon after graduating and eventually earned a law degree. He worked in the U.S. Treasury Department and became a trustee of Howard University. His son, Gale Hilyer, followed his father to the University of Minnesota and earned both bachelor's (1912) and law (1915) degrees. Gale practiced law for many years in Minneapolis, and among other distinctions he became, in 1930, the brother-in-law of Ralph Bunche when his wife's sister married the future United Nations ambassador and Nobel Peace Prize recipient.

In 1915, when Gale Hilyer first entered private practice, he joined the law firm of Albert Hall, a classmate of his father. It was a rare invitation for the time—an African American attorney being asked to join a white attorney's law firm—and perhaps gives added credence to the assessment of Andrew Hilyer's classmate that Hilyer "mingled with . . . almost perfect equality."

The most diligent keeper of statistics regarding African American higher education was the black community itself. Both the local and the national African American press were intensely interested in supporting and promoting education and reported frequently on black graduates and the successes of African American students. The longest-lived African American newspaper in the area, the *Appeal* (St. Paul), consistently noted a given year's graduates of area high schools and colleges. An article published in its pages in 1905 listed a total of seven African American graduates from the University of Minnesota up to that time, including Andrew Hilyer.

In 1910, educator and writer W. E. B. DuBois, who for many years edited the *Crisis*, the NAACP journal of African American sociology, literature, and politics, began publishing an annual report in the magazine on black graduates of higher education. Initially these surveys were devoted to the graduates of "Negro Colleges," which had sprung up, primarily in the South, during the years of Reconstruction following the Civil War and which served as the first choice of higher education for the great majority of black students across the United States.

During and after World War I, however, as African Americans began to migrate to industrial jobs in the North, increasing numbers of students began choosing northern state colleges. The *Crisis* reports reflect the change. The University of Minnesota made its first appearance in the annual tally in 1919. By 1923, it had eighteen African American students. There were twenty-six in 1924, thirty in 1925, and thirty-nine in 1928, including two graduates of the Medical School and one graduate of the School of Dentistry.

Black students at the university during its earliest days were certainly subject to racial stereotyping, some sanctioned by the academic institution itself. In the early 1910s, anthropology professor Albert Jenks openly and loudly espoused his theories on the "racial degradation" that would inevitably follow the miscegenation of an integrated society.

Personal slurs were common, too. Robert "Bobby" Marshall, who starred for the powerful Gopher football teams of 1904, 1905, and 1906 as an all-conference end, was described in the pages of the 1905 *Gopher* annual as a "lank-limbed child of sunny Ethiopia." Marshall was the first black athlete

Football star and multisport athlete Robert "Bobby" Marshall *(1905 Gopher annual)*

to play at the university and he was probably the first black athlete in the Western Conference, the forerunner of today's Big Ten. He went on to a legendary athletic career in the Twin Cities area, playing professional baseball and football, with a brief stint as a professional motorcycle racer thrown in for good measure.

For all the crudeness of the racial perspectives of the day, however, the small numbers of African American students at the university in these early times tended to isolate racial problems. It wasn't until the black student population on campus grew throughout the 1920s and became a community in its own right that segregationist elements around the university came fully to the fore and civil rights became an issue. Five African American co-eds were refused service at the Oak Tree Restaurant on Fourteenth Street near the campus in 1926, prompting a local black paper, the *St. Paul Echo*, to editorialize: "Racial discrimination, undoubtedly due to the larger registration of colored students this year and heretofore unheard of in any of the eating houses surrounding the campus, has definitely raised its head at the university."

It had raised its head earlier in the decade as well. In 1923, the *Minnesota Daily* reported that several Big Ten campuses were said to have Ku Klux Klan organizations within their student bodies. Though the story presented no evidence that a chapter existed at the University of Minnesota, the threat was serious. "That there are existing units of the Ku Klux Klan in St. Paul and Minneapolis has been known for some time," wrote the *St. Paul Pioneer Press* in a follow-up article to the *Daily* report. "Extension of the organization to the State University was not regarded with surprise by some alumni." University president Lotus Coffman issued a statement at the time, declaring that "action will be taken to squelch the order, if reports [of its existence] are found to be true."

Neither were classrooms immune to racism. In 1921, a political science professor named Jeremiah Young purposely omitted the name of an African American student, William Morrow, when he assigned seats for his class in alphabetical order. Professor Young subsequently told Morrow that he could sit in the back of the classroom, or to the side, but not elbow-to-elbow with his fellow students. Morrow stood up for his rights. He asked Professor Young to poll the other students in the class to see if they minded sitting next to him. They did not, and it was agreed that he should sit in proper alphabetical sequence. The story, which was reported in the *Minnesota Daily* the next day, also elicited an editorial from the paper titled "Minnesota for Whom?"

> Pitiful it seems that here at Minnesota—or at any other institution of learning—where we have whole departments devoted to Americanization and Sociology, to studies of American government and things allied, that anyone among us should take such an attitude [as Professor Young's]. Perhaps in the past, one or several students might have protested against being seated beside a colored student. It was then the duty of that professor to teach them that they were wrong, not to preserve the incident and apply it later.

Roy Wilkins was a university junior and had recently become the first black reporter at the *Daily* when the editorial appeared. There is no evidence that he wrote the piece, but Wilkins served on the campus newspaper staff for two years as a reporter and night editor. Wilkins would go on to fame as the longtime head of the NAACP and one of the leading figures in the nation's long struggle over civil rights. At the University of Minnesota, he was an outstanding student and a member of Omega Psi Phi fraternity, which became the first black organization ever to be pictured in a *Gopher* annual, in 1923.

Omega Psi Phi was not the only black fraternity on campus. The first, Pi Alpha Tau, came in 1911. There was also an Alpha Phi Alpha chapter. The first African American sorority on campus, Alpha Kappa Alpha, was established in 1922. In 1926, Alpha Kappa Alpha won the distinction of having the highest scholastic average of all the fraternity and sorority chapters on the campus.

Helen Jackson, of Minneapolis, who would become the sister-in-law of Roy Wilkins when she married his brother, Earl, was a Phi Beta Kappa student in 1928. Walter Minor and John Chenault graduated from the Medical School

Alpha Kappa Alpha, Eta Chapter, University of Minnesota, 1927

in 1930. The first black athletes since Bobby Marshall competed for the university in the late 1920s. They were Art Wiesager and William O'Shields, for the track team, and Ellsworth Harpole, who would become the first black Gopher football player since Marshall, in 1930. Vernon Wilkerson is thought to have been the first African American to earn his Ph.D. at the university, in agricultural biochemistry in 1932.

But for all of the successes of individual students, African American students, as a group and on the whole, did not share in the full life and benefits of a college education at the University of Minnesota. After Roy Wilkins and his fraternity brothers appeared in the 1923 *Gopher*, one can look in vain through the next dozen annuals for a photograph of an African American group or an individual African American among the numerous literary societies, professional groups, fraternities, sororities, and debating clubs that were such prominent features of the campus of the day.

Prospects for graduates were limited. Through the 1920s and 1930s, there were no African Americans hired to teach in any Twin Cities public schools. Employment of black graduates at a professional level in area businesses was virtually nonexistent. Talented male African American students favored professional degrees, like law and dentistry, that might allow them to earn a living within the black community, so that they did not have to rely on white society for income.

African American women were barred from one of the few professional opportunities open to women at the time. In 1925, President Coffman was contacted by the local head of the Women's Christian Association on behalf of a young, out-of-town student at the university named Dorothy Waters. Waters had applied to the school's nursing program and been accepted, only to be refused assignment at a St. Paul hospital because of the color of her skin. How could this happen? asked Mrs. James Paige.

"While the University of Minnesota has no prejudice against Miss Waters because she is colored," Coffman wrote, "nevertheless if we had known that she was colored we would have advised against her coming." The St. Paul hospital was a private facility. The university was only affiliated with it and did not control its personnel. "Those whom we send must be agreeable to the officers at the hospital."

The dean of the Medical School came closer to the crux of the matter in a letter of his own. When Waters arrived at the campus and it was learned that she was black, the nursing program "found [it] impossible to accommodate her because of the intimate work with white patients which our nurses have to undertake. You will note that the prejudice is not on our part at all but on the part of the patients."

* * *

Students changing classes during homecoming week, 1921

OVER THE NEXT TWO DECADES, as more African American students enrolled, the University of Minnesota would spend a good deal of time denying its own prejudice, even as it countenanced and supported the practices of racial discrimination. "Under the guise of doing what was best for all concerned, the University of Minnesota in the 1920s, '30s, and '40s often segregated black students and routinely denied them the full life of the campus," says Mark Soderstrom, who researched the history of the university's race relations for his University of Minnesota doctoral dissertation. "While the U of M was far from alone in its practices, and far from the worst transgressor in the ranks of colleges across the country, it was also slow to rectify the problems of racial inequality that became apparent on campus in the years before World War II."

The aim of segregation as practiced at the university, Soderstrom says, was to guard against troubles that would arise from the interaction of the races. To keep African Americans and whites from each other, "there was a very sophisticated mindset that mapped the way spaces were allocated. There was a space where [interaction] was appropriate and a space where it just couldn't happen."

Perhaps the most visible space where mixing could not happen was in the dormitories. It was a problem that first came to public attention in the fall of 1931 when freshman John Pinkett Jr. arrived at the newly opened Pioneer Hall. Pinkett, who was from Washington, D.C., had applied for and been accepted into the dormitory. But when he brought his bags to campus and authorities discovered he was African American, they suggested he look elsewhere for housing.

Coffman explained the matter in a letter to Lena Smith, president of the local NAACP: "John Pinkett, Jr., made a reservation in our university dormitory. The difficulties involved in this situation were pointed out to him. He stated that he preferred to live with those of his own color. Assistance was given to him in finding satisfactory accommodations." To Coffman, the separation of races was all a matter of common sense shared by African Americans and whites: "No rule has ever actually been adopted denying colored students admission to university dormitories. No colored student has applied before for admission to the U dorms. The good sense and sound judgment of the colored students and their parents with regard to this matter has been a source of constant gratification."

Of course, it was not so much good sense and sound judgment that kept African American students from applying for university housing. They knew they weren't welcome in dorms, or in the university-approved boarding-houses that surrounded the campus. Regarding these houses, a 1935 survey done by a student group, the All-University Council's Committee on Negro Discrimination, showed that of the sixty-two sanctioned dwellings, fifty-eight would not accept African Americans. Yet black students who applied to dorms were routinely given a list of these homes by the university, under the guise of helping them find alternative housing.

"There just wasn't any place to live on campus at the time," recalls Barbara Mallory Cyrus, who spent her years at the university commuting to school from the home she had grown up in on the north side of Minneapolis. "I think one group of young men lived in a rooming house in Dinkytown, above a drugstore. Otherwise, you either lived in a private home or at Phyllis Wheatley," a settlement house. Cyrus worked in the library at the settlement house, which, along with the Hallie Q. Brown Center in St. Paul, served as a social center for black university students. "We had fraternity and sorority dances [at Phyllis Wheatley] and basketball tournaments and plays."

Though no one kept precise numbers of students by race, a survey conducted by the All-University Council counted forty-five African Americans at the university in 1935. This included graduate students, many of whom had arrived in Minneapolis from southern black colleges.

According to Cyrus, the university at that time "was particularly welcoming of people studying social work. There were very limited job opportunities. Teaching wasn't a possibility, except in the southern schools. You couldn't teach locally. And, of course, no business or industry was hiring [black graduates]. Social work seemed to be a good out." A number of Minnesota social work students began filling the ranks of the Urban League, including Whitney Young (M.S.W. '47), who did his graduate work at the university and who would go on to fame as the national director of the league.

Meanwhile, housing problems continued to plague the university. In 1935, the All-University Council, in conjunction with its report on the state of African Americans on campus, asked President Coffman and the Board of Regents to allow blacks to integrate Pioneer Hall.

Coffman denied the request: "It is the unanimous opinion of the Board of Regents that the housing of Negro students in Pioneer Hall at present would not be conducive to their best interests, nor to the interests of the other students who may be residing there. The Regents recognize that deficiencies exist at the University with regard to housing and they wish to correct them as rapidly as possible for all students, including Negro students."

Although Coffman gave no indication in this public letter how the university planned to "correct" the housing deficiencies, in a private message to the All-University Council, Coffman suggested that the university and critics of its policy "do something constructive" to change it. His idea was to provide an "International House," which would offer rooms to African Americans only. Such houses were already in existence at Columbia University, the University of Chicago, and the University of California, Berkeley, according to Coffman. "I am wondering if the Council would be willing to join with me in making a study of this matter," he wrote. But no one seemed very interested in the idea at the time, or they were confused by the notion that an "international" house should be home to only African American students.

The local black press, the All-University Council, campus progressive groups, and, beginning in 1937, the first African American political group formed at the university, the Council of Negro Students, all clamored for change. But discriminatory practices continued, and not just in housing and not just on campus. This was an era in which touring black entertainers—renowned performers like Louis Armstrong and Duke Ellington—stayed in local homes because they couldn't find hotel rooms in the Twin Cities. It was an era when State Fair concessionaires routinely denied service to African Americans. There were few places on campus where black students could gather and few places nearby where they could meet. A number of local restaurants flatly denied tables to African Americans, offered slow service, or brought heavily salted food to the table.

In October 1935, the same month that Coffman and the regents issued their statement barring African Americans from the dorms, one of the period's most notorious moments of prejudice occurred. The Golden Gophers were preparing for the year's homecoming game. Minnesota's opponent was Tulane University of New Orleans. Walter White, secretary for the national office of the NAACP, outlined the controversy in a telegram sent to President Coffman a few days before the game:

Football player Dwight Reed was prevented from playing the 1935 homecoming game because Tulane University refused to play against African American athletes.

> National Association for Advancement of Colored People is informed that [Dwight] Reed, first string Negro end on University of Minnesota football team, will be kept out of Tulane game on October 19 because southern people oppose playing against Negro athletes (stop) We respectfully urge cancellation of game as rebuke to unsportsmanlike and prejudiced attitude of Tulane (stop) We do not believe University of Minnesota will surrender high principle for sake of gate receipts (stop) Cancellation of game would set high moral standard for other northern institutions in similar situations and would give growing number of fair-minded southern students encouragement in their efforts towards fair play (stop) I am sure you will agree University of Minnesota cannot descend to racial attitude of late Huey Long's state.

White's request fell on deaf ears. Despite local anger and national attention from the African American community, the game was played, and Dwight Reed watched from the press box.

Change would come, but it would come slowly. "It wasn't until people began to contest the system that said, 'this is where whites belong and this is where blacks belong' that things started to happen," says Soderstrom. "It was a small thing, but I think that one of the most revolutionary acts in the period was in January 1937, just after the formation of the Council of Negro Students. They went on a joint sledding party with a group of white students from the American Student Union. This kind of socializing was unheard of. There were probably deans rolling in their graves."

Barbara Cyrus is now retired from a long career as a Twin Cities editor. She first enrolled at the University of Minnesota in 1937 and joined the Council of Negro Students that fall. After spending her freshman year at Minnesota, Cyrus transferred to Spelman College in Atlanta, a black women's college, before returning to the University of Minnesota in the fall of 1939. The contrast between schools was sharp. "I was the only black student in my first three classes at the U that fall," she says.

One of the reasons that she chose to return to Minnesota after her year at Spelman was because the University Theater was planning to stage *Porgy and Bess* and she had been offered a role in the production. "I had seen two or three stagings of *Porgy* [including one starring Cab Calloway] and I thought it was just terrific that we were going to produce it here at the University," she says. It was to be the first all-black play on campus, which brought it a great deal of attention. In fact, *Life* magazine was considering using it as the subject of a photo essay.

But from the moment the staging of the play at the University was announced, it caused controversy within the local African American community. "First they complained about the language in the play," says Cyrus. "Then the people in the city heard about the staging and they got up in arms. We kept hearing this phrase, 'Detrimental to the race.'" *Porgy and Bess* was seen by many black people as a vehicle to promote racist stereotypes. Opponents of the production doubted that a white audience would grasp the fact that the characters in the play, and the play itself, were depictions and not a broad view of African American life.

"We do not dispute the existence of a 'Catfish Row' no more than we would dispute the existence of a 'Tobacco Road,' which portrays similar conditions among whites in the south," wrote editor Cecil Newman in the local paper, the *Minneapolis Spokesman*. "Unfortunately, most of those who see the play will not remember that it offers a social picture. They will tend to regard it as a typical illustration of Negro life everywhere." African American students of the day were "bound and determined to be seen as first-class citizens," Cyrus recalls. "We felt this intense pressure to always be perfectly groomed; to not be too loud or boisterous."

Porgy and Bess was ultimately canceled by the university, a fact applauded by its opponents as a sign of the growing influence of the black political voice in the community. That increased political voice also helped bring an end to Jim Crow housing. Its final days began in 1941, when the Phyllis Wheatley settlement house decided it would no longer take boarders, and the university felt obliged to find substitute housing for its black students. Lotus Coffman was dead, but his idea for an International House was resurrected to meet the new housing demands. The university purchased and refurbished a home on Washington Avenue and placed it in the charge of an African American graduate student, who rented rooms to a mix of white and black students. The university immediately shut the place down, claiming the house was meant for African American students only. The administration would sanction all-white facilities, like Pioneer Hall, and sanction all-black facilities, like an "International House," but a mix of students still violated its sensibilities.

Protests followed. Rallies on campus against the closing drew hundreds of protesters. Virtually every political group at the university, the local branches and national offices of the NAACP, and the African American community at large in the Twin Cities all protested the closing. Finally, it seemed the university would have to do something. "Times had changed," says Soderstrom. "The world was at war. This old form of segregation seemed suddenly unpatriotic."

The end of housing discrimination came with no great drama. Prompted by the protests, a committee was formed to look into the issue. Quietly the group agreed to open housing in the fall of 1942 to students of all races. It was typical of how racial conflicts were resolved during the period. The same structures of power that had instituted policies of segregation determined when they would end. Deeper issues would not be dealt with until another day.

In the postwar years, however, as the African American student body continued to grow, as it became more urban and more steeped in the passions of the civil rights movement, racial problems at the university would feel first a nudge and then a shove into the light of day.

A room party in the first women's dormitory, Sanford Hall, about 1910

A Place for Women

In November 1940, Ada Louise Comstock, president of Radcliffe College, returned to the University of Minnesota for the dedication of the second women's dormitory ever to be built on campus. Named in her honor, Comstock Hall opened its doors three decades after the inaugural women's residence, Sanford Hall, had been constructed with the guidance and support of the dean of women students at the University of Minnesota— Comstock herself.

It was only fitting that Comstock be chosen for the honor. Few American women in the first half of the twentieth century had had such a distinguished career in academic administration, few past female students at the University of Minnesota had a more successful professional life than this native of Moorhead, and no early administrator at the university did more than Comstock to strengthen the state of women and to secure for them a place—in both a literal and a figurative sense—on the campus of the University of Minnesota.

The university had changed in her absence. The student body had grown significantly, and so had the number of young women. Twenty-four years old when she began teaching at Minnesota, Comstock would later describe herself as "hardly older than the students." She was tall and good-humored and had a self-confidence boosted by the fact that she was the apple of her father's eye. "My father thought I was perfect from the day I was born," Comstock would later tell a researcher. "My mother had no such illusions."

Ada Comstock arrived at the University of Minnesota in 1892 as a bright sixteen-year-old freshman, the daughter of a successful lawyer and politician from the western prairies (Solomon G. Comstock served many years in the state legislature and one term in the U.S. Congress). She roomed with the family of an old friend of her father, Dean William Pattee of the Law School,

Ada Comstock, far left, with young friends, about 1890

and spent two years on the campus before moving on to Smith College in Northampton, Massachusetts, where she earned a bachelor's degree in 1897.

Comstock came back to Minnesota after graduation to earn another diploma—a teaching certificate from Moorhead Normal—before returning to the East in 1898. At Columbia University, Comstock earned a master's in English history and education, after which she headed once more to Minnesota, this time to assume her first academic position, in 1899: teaching English composition at the University of Minnesota under the watchful eye of the chair of the Department of Rhetoric, the venerable Maria Sanford.

As a young instructor, Comstock entertained a number of suitors—none of whom won her hand—and chafed at the occasionally overbearing presence of the department chair, Miss Sanford. She taught five classes a day and, in addition to those duties, quickly became an advocate for the wants and needs of the female students.

The most pressing of these was for space that women on campus could call their own. In the early days of the university, when female students had numbered in the dozens, a lounge had been set aside for their use in Old Main. By the turn of the century, when the number of women on campus was in the hundreds, that one room remained the only meeting area on campus that was exclusively theirs.

A Women's League formed at the university soon after Comstock's return to Minneapolis, with the expressed goal of trying to create a meeting place for women — one that would, in Comstock's words, "bring women students together in freer companionship." When Old Main burned in 1904, the need for this new facility became even more urgent. Ada Comstock soon became instrumental in league efforts, particularly in lobbying the president, Cyrus Northrop, to divert funds donated by Thomas Shevlin away from the construction of a chemistry building and toward the building of a women's center. Her efforts were successful, and in 1906 ground was broken for Shevlin Hall, which soon became the place on campus for women to dine, socialize, study, and meet.

Comstock's obvious gifts for advocacy on behalf of female students subsequently led to her appointment as the first dean of women, in 1907. This was a new role not only at the University of Minnesota but in higher education across the country. Just a handful of deans of women existed at state universities, and Ada Comstock quickly took on a leadership role in a national organization that formed among them.

She also set her sights on a next goal for the women of the university: a dormitory. At the time Comstock became the dean of women, there were more than one thousand female students, and the majority of them lived in

Shevlin Hall, built in 1906 as a place for women to study, dine, and socialize (1954 photograph)

Ada Comstock, president of Radcliffe College, about 1940

Minneapolis boardinghouses. Although many male students were also boarders, young, Victorian-era women put their reputations, if not their well-being, at risk for doing the same thing. There were a few sorority houses near campus as well, but Comstock was not a big fan of these: "Unless carefully regulated they often become such centers of gaiety as to be dangerous to the health and scholarship of those who live in them." Simply put, the off-campus circumstances of women were not, in her opinion, conducive to promoting collegial life. "A woman student at the University might live in complete isolation, gleaning from the college life only the benefits of the class-room," wrote Comstock, "or she might, if she were unfortunate in her choice of lodging house, suffer an absolute loss in refinement and in standards of behavior."

Again, Comstock's lobbying efforts, both at the university and now at the state legislature, were crucial for the creation of the first dormitory. In 1909, the state appropriated $100,000 for Sanford Hall, and construction began that very year. (Pioneer Hall, the first dorm for male students, was built in 1930.) The executive board of the all-female Student Government Association of the University of Minnesota—another innovation fostered by Comstock—expressed its thanks to Ada Louise Comstock through the *Shevlin Record*: "We are to have a girl's dormitory at Minnesota," the paper announced. "For her untiring work in procuring it, we as a board, which represents the girls whom it will benefit, thank Miss Comstock. We appreciate her friendship, her kindly assistance and advice during the year that is past."

Comstock continued to work on their behalf, finding scholarship funding for some students to help defray the costs of living in the dormitory and pushing for the construction of a women's gymnasium to help meet the health and recreation needs of her students. In this second goal she was not successful. Nor was she able to convince some male members of the community to take seriously the goals and aspirations of the female students of the University of Minnesota. At that 1940 dedication ceremony, Comstock gave a speech in which she recalled her early days at the university. It was a time when "the effort of women for higher education was still regarded as more or less a humorous thing, and occasion for jokes." She recalled visiting the editor in chief of one of the Minneapolis papers "to beg him sometimes to refer to women of the University of Minnesota by another term than coeds; and to write about their activities in a vein which was not facetious.

He laughed at me, I remember; and I haven't any recollection that my plea was ever seriously considered."

By 1912, her last year at the University of Minnesota, Ada Comstock had earned a stellar reputation, not just on campus but in academic circles around the United States. When her alma mater, Smith College, came calling, wanting to appoint her to its own brand-new deanship, she couldn't resist. Despite the entreaties of the new president at Minnesota, George Vincent, Comstock decided to head east, mainly because "she always loved taking a new job . . . and building it."

She would work at Smith for the next nine years, including one in which she served as the college's unofficial acting president — the trustees refused to grant her the official title because of her gender. Perhaps not surprisingly under these circumstances, she moved to Radcliffe in 1923, to become president of that college, a post she would hold for the next twenty years. Here again, Comstock's talents for negotiation and administration were instrumental. She was able to secure for Radcliffe its status as a sister school to a reluctant Harvard; at the same time, she promoted Radcliffe's standing as an independent women's college by expanding the graduate program and launching a nationwide admissions program.

Along with her academic work, Comstock was elected the first president of the American Association of University Women in 1921; she was the only woman selected to serve on the National Commission of Law Observance

Freshman in her dormitory window, probably Sanford Hall, about 1910 and Enforcement (known as the Wickersham Commission), where, among other duties, she worked for a repeal of the Eighteenth Amendment, which had established prohibition; and she was a vice chair of the Institute of Pacific Relations, an organization for which she reported on the Manchurian crisis of the 1930s, in the wake of the Japanese invasion of that country.

When Comstock retired from Radcliffe in 1943, at the age of sixty-seven, she surprised almost everyone who knew her by marrying an old friend whom she had first met at the University of Minnesota more than thirty years earlier. Wallace Notestein had been a young instructor in history when they first courted. He was an emeritus professor at Yale when he and Ada were finally married. They lived out the remaining years of their lives together in New Haven.

After Comstock died in 1973 at the age of ninety-seven, she was honored by Smith College in the form of the Ada Comstock Scholars Program, a prestigious program that helps fund nontraditional students at Smith. At the University of Minnesota, Comstock Hall remains as a reminder of Ada Comstock's work.

In fall 2005, the University of Minnesota instituted the Ada Comstock Distinguished Lecture Series. These free lectures, held twice a year, honor the exceptional research, scholarship, and leadership of female University of Minnesota faculty by featuring the work of these distinguished professors through their own words.

Ada Comstock would no doubt approve.

The Great Flu Epidemic and Ruth Boynton's Health Service

I N EARLY SEPTEMBER 1918, World War I was reaching its dreadful climax in the same fashion that it had begun: in unprecedented death and destruction. A reader scanning the news and preoccupied with images of the nation's soldiers donning gas masks and preparing for attack across "No Man's Land" could be forgiven for skipping past the page two headline from the September 12 *Minneapolis Tribune*. "Spanish Grippe Menace on East Coast Feared," it read.

The story was this: A strain of influenza, which had first appeared in a few army barracks in Kansas in early 1918, had crossed the ocean, inflicted armies and civilians in Europe, and picked up its nickname, "the Spanish flu." It was now back on the eastern seaboard of the United States, wreaking havoc in army camps from Boston to Washington, D.C., and threatening to spread to civilians. The report in the *Tribune* sounded somehow restrained: "Spanish influenza, although short-lived and of practically no permanent serious results, is a most distressing ailment which prostrates the sufferer during which he suffers the acme of discomfort."

But like the footsteps of some lumbering monster, the stories kept landing with a thud in the columns of the daily papers that September, sounding more and more ominous with each passing day. On the fifteenth, 1,000 cases of influenza were reported at a single camp outside of Boston. On the eighteenth, two more army camps were said to be ravaged by the flu. Three days later, that number had jumped to nine camps, and three days after that, more than 20,000 soldiers were reported sick with influenza.

Worse, this was not simply "a most distressing ailment." As the virus spread from the cantonments to the civilian population, "the acme of discomfort" was turning out to be death, in stunning numbers. More than 107 people died of influenza in Boston on a single day in late September. So

many were dying in Philadelphia that city morgues couldn't process the bodies.

Meanwhile, on the campus of the University of Minnesota, administrators were preparing for the beginning of a fall semester with a mission different from any the college had known before. A recently enacted draft law had stipulated that all able-bodied men between the ages of eighteen and forty-five were to be subject to conscription as of August 30, 1918. To process and train these new recruits, the federal government enlisted the help of colleges and universities across the country, including the U of M. By mid-September, two weeks before the start of school, the administration had enrolled more than 2,600 student draftees in a newly instituted program called the Student Army Training Corps (SATC).

An additional 3,000 soldiers, who were receiving training in a variety of military occupations, from mechanic to blacksmith to engineer, would also eventually fall under the aegis of the university's administration, making the University of Minnesota the single largest SATC center in the United States.

Somehow, the university was supposed to educate and train this boatload of new soldiers while at the same time continuing to function as an institution of higher education. Adding to the impending chaos: Fresh from the viral hot spots of Europe and the military camps of the eastern seaboard, a number of veterans of the war were coming to Minneapolis to oversee the military training of the newcomers.

By sheer coincidence, another new entity arrived on campus that fall. In mid-September, just as early reports of the dangers of the Spanish flu were drifting westward, the university announced that Dr. John Sundwall, from the University of Kansas, had been hired as the first director of the newly created University Health Service. Temporary space for the clinic was found in two vacated fraternity houses in the 1500 block of University Avenue Southeast. The week before school was set to begin, the Health Service opened for business.

Dr. John Sundwall, hired as director of the new University Health Service just weeks before the flu outbreak

It was an institution that had been years in the making. As early as 1904, a petition had been placed before the Board of Regents asking that "a fund for the care of sick students be created and used" to pay for hospital and medical care. A typhoid outbreak in southeast Minneapolis—one of many such scares in the city around the turn of the century—had prompted the request, and it was suggested that students be charged 50 cents a semester to cover the cost of the insurance. The Board of Regents said no to the idea of the fund, but it did urge the creation of a university health committee, which was duly constituted and immediately began to look into public health matters—particularly the quality of the university's water supply.

The health committee remained in existence after the initial typhoid panic, as did the idea, but not the reality, of a student health service. Another typhoid scare in late 1914 prompted the revival of health committee activities, which would ultimately include an attempt to survey and systematize the teaching of public health at the university. The committee urged that typhoid and smallpox vaccinations be given students at no cost and called for another examination of university water sources and uses.

But still no health service, until Marion Leroy Burton arrived on campus as the newly appointed president in 1917. While serving as president of Smith College, Burton "had shown much interest in provisions for adequate health-medical services for students," according to a brief history of the beginnings of the health program, written by Sundwall. Burton brought that interest to Minnesota and quickly became an advocate for a campus health office.

By October 1917, Burton had asked the regents if $5,000 of the university budget could be designated for the service. Students would be asked to contribute $3 per semester for use of the system, and most of the university's contribution would be dedicated to the salary of a director. The regents agreed to the plan that winter, and by summer 1918 Burton was leading the search for a head doctor. Sundwall was hired just before the start of the school year.

As reports of the epidemic on the East Coast were growing more ominous and the SATC reported for duty, there was a feeling of deep uneasiness at the new University Health Service. "Influenza having reached Boston we felt certain that it would soon show up at the University of Minnesota among our Student Army Training Corps. Military officers—from abroad and all parts of our land—were reporting almost daily to conduct drills and offer instruction," wrote Sundwall. "Nothing could be more favorable for the introduction and spread of this contagion."

On September 27, the Minnesota State Board of Health received its first two notices of influenza. The very next day, seven cases of flu were reported in North Branch, one hundred cases in the town of Wells, twenty-one cases at Fort Snelling, and thirty cases at the University Hospital, including twenty-one nurses. In a matter of hours, the newly inaugurated University Health Service was wall-to-wall students. According to Sundwall, "There were incessant calls for help."

The SATC was hit first. Crammed into improvised barracks at the old Exposition Building near St. Anthony Falls, the student soldiers lived in the sort of elbow-to-elbow proximity that made the spread of infection a certainty. And, unfortunately, there wasn't much that anyone could do once the virus struck. "Two things in connection with the pandemic are indelibly impressed on my memory," wrote Sundwall. "The one was the characteristic chain of symptoms—sudden onset; fever; extreme prostration; pains in back, head, and extremities; involvement of the respiratory system, and early pneumonia in a large percentage of cases. The other impression was the helplessness of the medical sciences."

Given the fears generated by the bloody news from the front in Europe, the patriotic press continued to downplay the bad news that a plague of influenza had descended upon the land. Headlines about the gravity of the flu one day would be followed the next by optimistic pronouncements about a "waning" epidemic. In fact, it was impossible to cover up the breadth of the epidemic. One thousand cases of the flu were reported in Minneapolis by the end of the first week of the outbreak. In addition, obituaries of local servicemen and of Red Cross nurses in Europe and camps in the United States—dead from influenza or from the pneumonia that was an offshoot

of the virus—were scattered throughout the pages of the paper. And from the East Coast, reports of the health crisis were shocking. As many as 2,600 Philadelphians died from the flu in the first week of October; the next week, the total topped 4,500.

On September 29, university president Burton announced that the fall opening of the University of Minnesota would be postponed for one week, "as a measure of precaution" against the spread of the disease. A week later, that postponement was extended a week, and it would be pushed back one final time before the month was through. On October 7, 140 new civilian cases were reported in Minneapolis, along with 8 deaths. On October 11, the city closed churches, schools, theaters, dance halls, and all other meeting places for the duration of the epidemic.

Meanwhile, the newly opened health clinic was seeing 100 patients a day. When Health Service quarters became too crowded, students were looked after in their dorm rooms and barracks. Many were already desperately ill before they arrived at the converted fraternity houses on University Avenue. "I shall never forget the first victim at the University," wrote Sundwall, "a

Elbow-to-elbow living conditions for the Student Army Training Corps helped spread the flu virus.

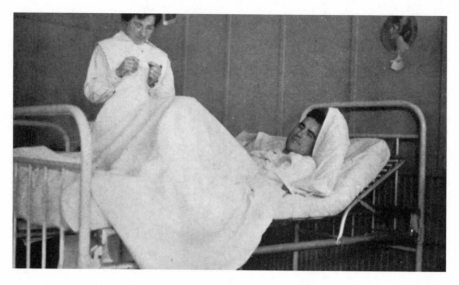

The University Health Service, which was housed in converted fraternity houses on University Avenue, treated flu victims as school opened, 1918.

handsome, robust young second lieutenant. In less than a week his body was sent home."

Sundwall enlisted medical help from the University Hospital, but the work itself was extremely hazardous. One of the October 7 victims of influenza, Edward Slater, was a 1918 graduate of the University Medical School who had been assisting at the clinic. A second doctor, A. G. Alley (M.D. '05), would also succumb to "pneumonia following influenza" after helping at the clinic.

By the end of the black month of October 1918, the influenza had waned just enough for the university to open its doors to students. The worst of the crisis came in the clinic's first two months of existence, but the epidemic ebbed and flowed through February 1919. In all, during its first fall and winter of duty, the health clinic treated more than 2,000 cases of influenza that resulted in 20 deaths. (A second outbreak of a related influenza virus struck with consequences nearly as gruesome the following school year.)

As for the overall toll of the pandemic: It was awesomely brutal. In all of recorded history, including the Black Death of the Middle Ages, there has never been a more deadly outbreak. Estimates of the victims worldwide range from a very conservative 20 million to upward of 200 million. In the United States, more than 600,000 died. So many of the dead were so young that the average life expectancy in the country dropped from 51 years in 1917 to 39 years by the end of 1918.

In time, health professionals would learn that this particular virus triggered a response so massive that the immune system of a victim could destroy the sufferer's lungs as it attacked the virus. Those with the strongest immune systems, people between the ages of 18 and 40, were the most likely to die. In fact, a curve charting the deaths by age groups would eventually be graphed in the shape of a W, whose peaks represented the deaths of infants, young adults, and the elderly.

No one has ever done a comprehensive assessment of the toll the pandemic took on University of Minnesota graduates and students. A simple count of the cause of death of 81 victims of the war memorialized in the 1920 *Gopher* annual shows that at least 15 succumbed to influenza. Along with the 20 who died on campus in the fall and winter of 1918–19 and another 16 who succumbed to the flu or pneumonia in 1919–20, those victims with an immediate or known connection to the university total 51. But in addition, the lists of the deceased in the *Minnesota Alumni Weekly* during the fall and early winter were lengthy and heartbreaking; and there were certainly many more victims who had no present connection to the campus or the war effort.

For all of this, the student body at the University of Minnesota turned out to have been luckier than most. It had far fewer cases of influenza and a lower mortality rate than many other institutions across the country. In a grim annual report given to the president the next spring, the Health Service reported that "100 deaths might reasonably have been expected. Under the conditions students were infinitely better off here than at home. From the standpoint of urgent need the University Health Service was organized at a most opportune time."

By the end of December 1918, a little more than a month after Armistice Day, the Student Army Training Corps was dismantled and troops were either sent home or stationed elsewhere. The fraternities on University Avenue were soon reoccupied by students, and the Health Service was forced to move to offices on the first floor of Pillsbury Hall in February 1919.

In due time, full activity returned to the campus, and health care would continue to be a service provided to the students. As for its beginnings, President Burton would write: "There seemed something almost providential about getting the Health Service started just in time to serve during that pandemic."

RUTH BOYNTON had just arrived on the campus of the University of Minnesota as a newly enrolled medical student when she made her first acquaintance with the institution that would become the center of her professional universe in years to come. It was that awful autumn of 1918, and Boynton quickly contracted the dread influenza and found herself being treated, along with hundreds of others, at the newly created Student Health Service. A native of La Crosse, Wisconsin, and a recent graduate of the University of

Ruth Boynton, youthful director of the University Health Service, 1936

Wisconsin in Madison, Boynton was one of the lucky ones who survived the ordeal. Perhaps out of appreciation for the aid she received there, Boynton returned to the Health Service in 1921 with her medical degree in hand to begin a long and distinguished career in student health.

With the exception of a couple of brief stints early in her career when she served as director of the Division of Child Hygiene for the State of Minnesota and then taught at the University of Chicago, Boynton would spend her next forty years in the employ of the University Health Service. In 1936, she became the first woman in the nation to be appointed the director of such a service, and she would hold that post for twenty-five years.

Boynton was at the University Health Service as the U of M grew from a good-sized land grant institution in the years prior to World War II into a huge state university. She was there as GIs poured into college after the war; and she was there through the continued growth of the university in the 1950s. She oversaw the commensurate growth of the Health Service, which had begun as a one-doctor unit housed in a few rooms in the basement of Pillsbury Hall and wound up, by the time of her retirement, as one of the most essential and important services offered by the university to its students, faculty, and employees.

After its horrible first days in 1918, dealing with the Spanish flu, the Health Service settled into the routine of handling more typical student health problems. It also quickly experienced its first growth spurt. In 1921, the same year that Boynton was hired, John Sundwall took the position of director of Health Services at the University of Michigan and was replaced as director by Dr. Harold Diehl. Dr. William Shepard was hired as the third and final full-time M.D. on this staff.

The most pressing ongoing concern of the service at the time was tuberculosis. The university averaged two new cases of TB a month during these early years of the Health Service. But as with all student health services, the most frequent misery attended to was the common cold, and Boynton, Shepard, and Diehl spent long hours not just prescribing bed rest and aspirin but looking for a cure.

According to Shepard, in a recollection published at the time of Boynton's retirement, a post–World War I report from a weapons arsenal in Maryland suggested that workers in the plant who had been engaged in making chlorine bombs for gas warfare "were remarkably free of colds." This prompted an experiment at the University of Minnesota in which a group of students with colds were sent to a "chlorine room." "A very small, carefully measured amount of chlorine" was pumped into the room. Afflicted students would sit for an hour in study chairs, breathing the chlorinated air. Its effectiveness as a remedy for the sniffles was then matched against the more traditional treatment given another group. The chlorine cure didn't work, but under Diehl and then Boynton, the Health Service would continue to conduct a number of experiments in the vain hope of finding that ever-elusive fix for the common cold.

Shepard also reveals that in the first years of the Health Service there was "a terrific outbreak of scarlet fever at the farm [St. Paul] campus." But its most serious crisis was an epidemic of smallpox that struck the Twin Cities in the mid-1920s. Eight thousand vaccinations were given to students and other members of the university community; still, seven students contracted the disease and died.

Boynton's initial foray into the world of student health whetted her appetite for continued service. In 1927, she earned her master's degree in public health from the university and subsequently taught at the University of Minnesota, as well as at the University of Chicago. Along with public health, she was interested in the study of tuberculosis. TB remained the largest and most feared killer of college-age students when Boynton assumed the role of director. While in that position, she would expand the amount of TB testing done at the university, insisting first that all new students be tested for the disease and then that all staff, academic and nonacademic, be tested as well. It was one of the early steps in what would become a gradual process of expanding the Health Service from its focus on students to its ultimate role as a university-wide service.

In 1936, Boynton replaced Diehl, who left to become dean of the Medical School and who would do much to build the national reputation of that institution. He turned over to Boynton a service that had grown to nine full-time physicians, twenty-eight part-time doctors, eleven part-time dentists, and a whole slew of nurses, administrators, and other staff. The Health Service had long since left Pillsbury Hall and was now housed in a wing of the University Hospital. It cared for a potpourri of health needs for the four to five hundred students it saw on a daily basis.

Aside from the TB testing, Boynton instituted some immediate changes at the Health Service. Consultants in proctology and urology were added at the service, as well as "a diet table," which focused on students with diabetes, nephritis, gastric ulcers, and colitis. Boynton's early concern about what students ate foreshadowed the modern era. Her "diet table" primarily treated obese students, who had trouble finding healthy foods elsewhere on the campus or in Dinkytown restaurants. She hired a graduate student

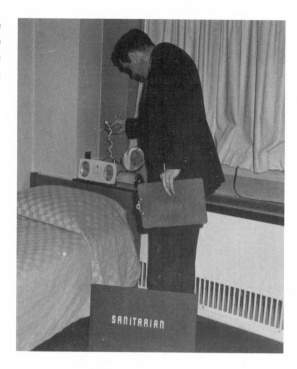

Health service
sanitarian
inspecting safety in
campus housing

dietician to oversee the menus at the table, and eighty-two students signed up for the service in its first year.

Another problem was the excessive use of Benzedrine by students on campus. First introduced around 1940, the drug quickly became popular around exam time for students looking for post-midnight boosts. One year, Boynton and the Health Service had four students in the hospital suffering from Benzedrine overdoses. In response, the Health Service ran an ad in the *Minnesota Daily* informing students of the dangers of the drug. "Whether this was effective, I do not know," Boynton would later write a colleague. In any case, the initial popularity of the drug faded and there were no more cases of overdose.

Beginning in her early years at the service and continuing throughout, Boynton would respond to an increasing number of "mental hygiene" problems at the university. Particularly in the postwar years, Boynton oversaw the boosting of psychiatric and psychological counseling services for students, including increasing aid to a number of vets dealing with what would come to be called post-traumatic stress.

World War II and its aftermath brought other special problems to the University Health Service. During the war, as the campus became home to a large number of servicemen, the incidence of communicable diseases increased. Particularly frightening was a November 1943 outbreak of influenza. For those, like Boynton herself, who had lived through the 1918 pandemic, the week of November 22, when Coffman Union was converted into an emergency hospital and eighty beds were set up in the halls of the building, must have seemed terribly frightening. This strain of flu was not deadly, however, and the epidemic passed in four weeks with no fatalities. (A far more serious outbreak of influenza came in 1957 — 1,200 University of Minnesota students wound up hospitalized with the disease. Fortunately, once again there were no deaths.)

The years after the war saw an enormous boost in student enrollment on campus and a corresponding jump in visits to Health Service offices. From just under 40,000 trips to the Minneapolis clinic in 1944–45, the service had to handle more than double that number (a total of 81,715) in 1946–47. To meet these demands, both full- and part-time staff were increased, including the addition of three physicians and two full-time psychiatrists. Administration became much more complex as the service now had to deal with veterans attending the university under the auspices of the GI Bill. The Veterans Administration contracted with the University Health Service to provide campus medical services for its ex-soldiers, adding to the administrative and medical burdens of the service.

Not surprisingly, given the circumstances, the beds and waiting rooms at the old health center (in Minneapolis, still housed at University Hospital) quickly proved inadequate to the growing needs of the university, and plans were made to construct a new building. Dental care, the eye clinic, and record room offices, which had moved to another location in 1946, were reunited with the rest of the clinic only after the new clinic was finished in the fall of 1950. The four-story structure was built across from a wing of the hospital on Church Street, in the heart of the campus. In conjunction with a service on the St. Paul campus, Dr. Boynton pronounced that "the University of Minnesota now has physical facilities for its Health Service second to none."

But student numbers kept rising, and student services were expanded. In 1954, Boynton hired a full-time health educator and enlarged both the pharmacy and X-ray departments at the service. Also housed in the building under the administration of the Health Service was the university's Environmental Health Department. Just five years after the new Health Service was completed, another expansion was needed.

By all accounts, Boynton not only kept pace with the dizzying rate of change at the university but also generously offered her expertise to the wider world of public health. Boynton was active in state public health matters as well. For twenty-two years she served on the Minnesota State Board of Health and was twice elected its president. From 1931 until her retirement, she was a professor of preventive medicine and public health at the university, and she served as acting director of the School of Public Health during World War II. In addition, in the early 1950s, a Rhodes scholarship took her to Oxford for a year, where she assisted British colleges in establishing student health services.

When she retired in 1961, Boynton was one of the most highly regarded directors of student health programs in the country. She moved to Miami, where she lived with a companion, Prudence Cartwright, and worked as the unpaid secretary-treasurer for the American Student Health Association. According to her old colleague, Dr. William Shepard, who visited her in her new home, "She seems to be enjoying the happiest days of her life."

In 1975, the University of Minnesota honored her long and distinguished career by renaming its health service for her. Boynton herself was able to attend the ceremony, but she lived just two more years. The Boynton Health Service still carries her name.

Geniuses and Characters

General Custer's 1874 expedition discovered gold near French Creek, but geology professor N. H. Winchell doubted the find's significance.

General Custer and the
Geology Professor

O N JULY 2, 1874, George Armstrong Custer led a large caravan of Seventh Cavalry troops, Arikara Indian scouts, and civilian teamsters, including Calamity Jane, toward the Black Hills from Fort Lincoln in the Dakota Territory. Along for the ride were a couple of miners, a handful of newspaper correspondents and scientists, a St. Paul photographer, and two members of the University of Minnesota faculty—geology professor N. H. Winchell and rhetoric professor A. B. Donaldson. As if scripted by John Ford, the first giddyap of the assemblage was done to the tune of "Garry Owen," by a sixteen-piece brass band that Custer was pleased to bring along as well.

This was *not* to be Custer's last expedition from Fort Lincoln. That would come in two years' time and would end, as we all know, in a hail of arrows and bullets at Little Big Horn. But much of what Custer did during his years on the plains, including this strange journey, seems laden with portent.

The trip was made at the behest of the U.S. Army. Its stated objective—"to examine the country in and about the North Fork of the Sheyenne, shown on the maps as the Belle Fourche: also, the country south of it in the vicinity of Bear Butte, commonly known as the Black Hills"—doesn't tell the half of it. Custer was steering his forces toward ground sacred to Plains Indians, and everyone from Bismarck to Washington, D.C., knew it. In a treaty whose ink was just six years old, the federal government and representatives of the Sioux (Dakota and Lakota), Cheyenne, and Arapaho people had agreed in no uncertain terms that white settlers would never "be permitted to pass over, settle upon, or reside in the territory described in this article."

The land so designated was centered upon the Black Hills. The problem was that in 1874, the westward expansion of white settlement was sweeping through Minnesota into the Dakota Territory. Boosters in hamlets along

STEREOGRAPHS OF THE BLACK HILLS.
Photographed by W. H. Illingworth.

George Custer's 1874 expedition of cavalry, scouts, and two university professors
(stereoscope photo by William H. Illingworth)

PUBLISHED BY W. H. ILLINGWORTH.

No   East Seventh Street St Paul. Minn.

No. 852.   Custer's Expedition.

Young geology professor Newton H. Winchell, given the task of conducting Minnesota's first geological and natural history survey

the upper reaches of the Missouri River, from Yankton to Bismarck, were clamoring to have Native American land opened for white settlers.

Enhancing this itch was the fact that for years the Black Hills had been rumored to be full of gold. There were stories stretching back almost fifty years, of white adventurers trekking into the hills, finding fortunes, and then losing their lives and riches to Native Americans protecting the sanctity of the hills the Lakota called Paha Sapa. Though no one had ever trekked out of the region with pockets full of gold, the legend persisted.

In 1873, the United States sank into a severe economic depression. A gold strike in the Black Hills would surely help stabilize the economy—or so the argument went. Though most interested white Americans understood that any encroachment on the Black Hills would goad various Siouan bands into a fight, many of them simply didn't care. The *Bismarck Tribune* spoke in the language of a brutal Realpolitik when it wrote on the occasion of Custer's departure: "The American people need the country the Indians now occupy; many of our people are out of employment; the masses need some new excitement. The war is over, and the era of railroad building has been brought to a termination by the greed of capitalists and the folly of grangers; and depression prevails on every hand. An Indian war would do no harm, for it must come, sooner or later."

The U.S. Army could innocently claim that it was just heading into the Black Hills to see what it could see. But to most observers, the expedition creaked and rattled across the plains to settle a couple of big issues: Was there, or was there not, gold in those hills? And what would the Plains Indians do if their territory was suddenly swamped with white people?

Of course, the preferred answer to the first question—at least in the booster camp—was a resounding "Yes!" And to help promote this desire, the gold interest managed to send along two miners, experienced in the Colorado gold rush of the 1860s and inclined to believe in El Dorado whether they saw it or not. Their names were Horatio Ross and William McKay, and, in the words of one historian, "if [either one] were officially attached to the command, nobody ever admitted."

The person who would ultimately offer a more sober, scientific judgment of the mineral value of the Black Hills was the expedition's only professional geologist: Newton Horace Winchell, of the University of Minnesota. In time, Winchell would become one of the most esteemed scientists in

Minnesota history. When he headed out with Custer and the others from Fort Lincoln in 1874, however, Winchell was nothing but a greenhorn "bug catcher," in the parlance of the weathered soldiers who guarded his backside as he gathered samples. Never mind that he collected quartzite rather than monarch butterflies.

Winchell had arrived in Minnesota two years earlier, after earning undergraduate and master's degrees in geology from the University of Michigan, where his brother, Alexander, chaired the Departments of Geology, Zoology, and Botany. Prior to coming to Minnesota, Winchell had done geological and botanical fieldwork in Ohio, Michigan, and New Mexico. He had also served as a school superintendent in Michigan. The job at the University of Minnesota was his first college teaching post, and it came with an added duty. In the same year that the university hired Winchell, President William Watts Folwell and the state government joined forces to create Minnesota's first Geological and Natural History Survey. Winchell was hired to head both the survey and the tiny Geology Department, which in 1872 consisted solely of N. H. Winchell.

In an era in which the great white pine forests of the Upper Midwest were being toppled in massive swaths, the tall grass prairie was fast being turned by the plow, buffalo were nearing extinction, and the passenger pigeon was forever vanishing from this earth, it might be uplifting to assume that these early zoological, botanical, and geological surveys were created in the spirit of conservation. In fact, the idea of conservation was so new in 1872 that the word, in its present connotation, had yet to be invented.

Most enterprising Minnesotans of the day—like their white neighbors in the Dakota Territory—were far more interested in a survey that would tell them what riches might be hauled off the land rather than how many species of birds inhabited Minnesota or just when the last glacier of the last ice age receded. The geological portion of the survey legislation, for instance, required that it be conducted "with a view to a complete account of the mineral kingdom as represented in the state . . . [and] the value of said substances for economical purposes and their accessibility."

In addition to cataloging the mineral kingdom and its value, the survey was expected to offer a full rundown of the state's plant and animal life, compile meteorological data regarding Minnesota's weather, create an accurate state map, and establish a natural history museum at the university. For all of these chores, the legislature set aside a grand total of $1,000, apparently expecting, in the words of one historian, "a large share of the work to be done by good fairies."

Winchell was asked by the U.S. Army to perform a more limited function on his trip with Custer. He was to do a geological survey of the Black

Hills and the region through which the wagon train would be passing. As Winchell understood it, that meant an examination of as much of the "mineral kingdom" as he could study in the two months of the expedition. It didn't mean that he was supposed to look for gold.

The university's other faculty member on the expedition, rhetoric professor Aris B. Donaldson, was moonlighting. The *Saint Paul Daily Pioneer* had hired Donaldson to serve as its correspondent for the trip. He joined journalists from Chicago, Bismarck, and New York and from the *Pioneer*'s rival, the *St. Paul Press*, in making a lively press corps that fed reports of the expedition back east throughout the summer.

It took three weeks for the party to wend its way south and west to the Black Hills. At fifteen to thirty miles a day, the pace was brisk for foot soldiers, teamsters, and Winchell, who was frantically trying to gather scientific data. But for others, there was an element of idyll to the journey. There were just two encounters with small bands of Indians through the whole course of the trip. A couple of baseball games were organized once the party got to the Black Hills. Donaldson and others described breathtaking vistas and valleys so rich in flowers of every color that even the hard-living teamsters were moved to decorate their wagons with bouquets.

Custer was an avid big-game hunter who always traveled with a kennel of wolfhounds. He seems to have spent much of the trip heading out ahead of the rest of the party to shoot elk, deer, a crane, and—much to his delight, for he had never killed one before—a grizzly bear. According to Evan Connell in his classic study *Son of the Morning Star*, Custer had become enamored with the art of taxidermy on a trip to Yellowstone the summer before, in 1873. Although there is no reference to him practicing his skills on this journey, he did send specimens—including the crane—back to Central Park in New York for preservation. He bestowed a similar gift on the University of Minnesota. A group of Santee scouts in the party killed three large elk. According to Winchell's field notes of the trip, Custer allowed him to send one of the elk skins back to the university's nascent Museum of Natural History for mounting. Ever the geologist, Winchell notes: "Where we skin the elks the rock is a very fine-grained, greenish chlorite slate."

Once in the Black Hills, the party spent a week and a half exploring the region. Winchell did the best he could, in this brief stay, to catalog the shale, slate, clay, gypsum, sandstone, limestone, and granite that the hills contained. The two miners in the party, Ross and McKay, went looking for gold. On July 30, near French Creek, they found 10 cents' worth. In his field notes, Winchell's only comment on the matter is brief and perhaps a little skeptical: "The gold-seekers who accompany the expedition report the finding of gold in the gravel and sand along [French Creek]."

Beer and a meal in the shade on the 1874 expedition (President Ulysses S. Grant's son, Fred Grant, at right)

However laconic Winchell was about the discovery, the camp was abuzz. When more gold turned up on August 1 in a location a few miles away, a mini-rush occurred within the party; soon soldiers, cooks, sutlers, and teamsters were out prospecting for gold. Though they didn't find much, that didn't stop Custer from deciding to broadcast the news that gold had been discovered in the Black Hills. A scout named Charley Reynolds was sent to the telegraph station at Fort Laramie, in what is now Wyoming, and before the rest of the party was halfway home to Fort Lincoln, the whole world had heard the news. "STRUCK IT AT LAST," screamed the headline of the *Yankton Press and Dakotian*. "Rich Mines of Gold and Silver Reported Found by Custer. PREPARE FOR LIVELY TIMES."

There is no record of Winchell doing anything to dampen Custer's—or anyone's—enthusiasm for gold. But if he was inclined to do so, he had ample opportunity to bend the general's ear. The day after the first strike, Winchell, Donaldson, Custer, and a couple of others spent a challenging day together climbing the highest mountain in the Black Hills, Harney Peak. At one point in the journey, Winchell and Custer were by themselves, trying to scale what turned out to be a false summit. "We found here a long, narrow ridge of bare rock, along which we passed," writes Winchell, "occasionally coming to broken-down spots that had to be crossed by letting each other down and helping each other up." Whatever the professor and the general may have chatted about in this intimate moment is lost forever in the canyons of the Black Hills.

As it turned out, no one in the party was able to climb to the summit of the mountain. Still they commemorated the ascent by jamming a note with their names and the date in an empty cartridge shell and driving the shell into the seam of a rock. Winchell took samples and noted that the peaks were composed of "a gray or white feldspathic granite." Donaldson asked Winchell and Custer to check their pulse rates and reported Winchell's at 136 per minute and Custer's at a healthier 112.

AFTER ANOTHER WEEK in the Black Hills, the party headed for home. On August 30, Custer and the expedition returned to Fort Lincoln as it had left, to the tune of "Garry Owen." According to Connell, "Ree [Arikara] scouts led the parade, wearing their best moccasins, leggings, and calico shirts. Next came the staff officers, the band, the trumpeters. Women, children, and members of the garrison came running out from the fort" to greet them.

It is safe to say by the time Newton Winchell got back to Minnesota, in early September, only a handful of people were interested in the substance of his report, which dealt primarily with the shales, slates, and limestones

of the Black Hills. Everywhere in the country the word had spread: There was gold in the Dakota Territory. Newspapers across the Middle West were already clamoring for the government to take the Black Hills from the Indians. By October, the first gold rushers were sneaking into Paha Sapa.

Nonetheless, Winchell stirred controversy with a brief passage in his report when it was published in the *New York Tribune* in mid-September. After listing all of the rocks that composed the Black Hills, he essentially reiterated his flat statement from his notes on the day gold was found in French Creek. Then he threw in a clinker: "The miners that accompanied the expedition report the finding of gold and silver in the south-eastern portion of the Hills, though I saw none of the gold nor did I see any auriferous quartz. I have taken the gold reports with a large grain of allowance."

Winchell's doubts were given credence in a few quarters in Washington and New York, where a more cautious approach to westward expansion prevailed. But in the Dakota Territory, Winchell's text was sneered at. "If Professor Winchell has made such reports," the *Bismarck Tribune* wrote, "he has written himself an ass." Custer himself weighed in on the topic in a letter to the *New York World* a few months after the height of the controversy. "Why Professor Winchell saw no gold," he wrote succinctly, "was simply due to the fact that he neglected to look for it."

That was true enough. And, in fact, history would prove Winchell wrong and the others right. There was plenty of gold in the Black Hills. But, of course, it would be mined at a steep price to Native Americans, as well as to the man who led that ominous expedition into the Black Hills. Paha Sapa would never be the same after Custer's trip. As prospectors started flocking

Winchell's canoe, used during the Geological Survey, in front of Pillsbury Hall, 1878 into the Black Hills, Lakota leaders like Sitting Bull, Crazy Horse, and Gall began gathering their people to drive the white men away. It was ostensibly to protect the lives and limbs of trespassers that the Seventh Cavalry went back to the region in 1876. Custer and almost three hundred others would never return from the assignment.

Though it's certain that Newton Horace Winchell had some thoughts on these subsequent events, he didn't put them to paper. Winchell had much work to do in Minnesota, where his legacy was left undamaged by the expedition. In a career that spanned more than forty years, he would do more than his share to write the geological and archaeological histories of the state. His studies of St. Anthony Falls helped judge the rate of the falls' recession and defined the glacial epochs that shaped the Upper Midwest. His work in the iron ranges of northern Minnesota alerted miners to the fact that there was more than one iron field in the Arrowhead region and helped make of that area a kind of gold mine in itself. For almost thirty years, he headed the Geological Survey for the State of Minnesota, and when he retired from that job, Winchell joined the State Historical Society as its chief archaeologist, where he proceeded to write a mammoth tome on Native American archaeology, *The Aborigines of Minnesota*.

He was a founding member of the Minnesota Academy of Sciences and, along with his brother, Alexander, created and edited the journal the *American Geologist*. Two of his sons became prominent geologists in their own right and a daughter married one of the sons of the founder of Dayton's Department Store. In 1988, the University of Minnesota renamed its Earth Sciences Department the Newton Horace Winchell School of Earth Sciences to honor his many achievements in geology.

Aris Donaldson, the university rhetoric professor on the expedition, apparently found journalism to his liking. A year after the expedition, he bought the *Alexandria Post* in Minnesota and served as its publisher and editor until his death in 1883.

As for the elk that Custer bestowed on the Natural History Museum, apparently it had company. When the Bell Museum opened in 1939, its first director, Thomas Sadler Roberts, wrote a report in which he outlined the early days of the Bell's antecedent, the Natural History Museum, created by the Minnesota legislature in 1872. The first museum was housed in Old Main and included, according to Roberts, "mammals, collected in the Black Hills by the Custer Expedition." These had been sent to "Ward, of Rochester, to be mounted" and "consisted of two antelopes, male and female, a deer with young, an elk head, a badger, a grizzly bear with young, a weasel, and [also sent to Ward] a large moose killed in eastern Otter Tail County in December, 1874."

In the years that followed, the growing museum moved to a succession of locations across campus, and once, in 1885, much of it was shipped to New Orleans for a temporary exhibit. By the early part of the century, the total number of skins and mounted specimens owned by the museum numbered in the thousands. When Roberts took charge of the institution in 1915, he disposed of a large number of decaying specimens. Though, in his 1939 report, Roberts doesn't say exactly what became of the Black Hills collection, this is likely how it vanished. It is no longer a part of the museum collection.

ONE FINAL FOOTNOTE on Custer and the Natural History Museum. When her husband was killed at Little Big Horn, Custer's widow, Elizabeth, received custody of his hounds. She gave one of these to an old friend of her husband, a Minneapolis minister named C. M. Terry, who kept the dog until its death. At that time, Terry sent it over to the museum to be mounted—perhaps thinking it might join the elk and grizzly bear in a Black Hills tableau. The wolfhound, named Cardigan, was duly preserved and kept in the collections until it, too, became a little musty. T. S. Roberts was about to dispose of the animal, at about the same time he was cleaning out the other specimens in the museum, when Cardigan disappeared.

In May 1923, the *Minneapolis Tribune* tried to trace the poor dog's whereabouts. The strongest rumor, according to the paper, suggested that a janitor took it and sold it to a "dime museum" in Minneapolis, where others reported seeing it exhibited until the museum finally shut down. Just where it went from the dime museum is a little foggy, and the final resting place of Cardigan's remains is unknown. To this day, curators at the Bell field inquiries about its fate.

View of the university in 1904, not long after J. Frank Wheaton set up practice in Manhattan with an African American attorney who had practiced in Minnesota. The campus buildings (from left) are Nicholson, Eddy, and the smoking remains of Old Main. At right is Jones Hall, known as the Physics Building.

"A Spectacular Career"

IT WAS MID-MAY 1900, and Minnesota's Republican Party was gathered for a political lovefest at the Exposition Building in Minneapolis. The state GOP, assembled to choose representatives for the upcoming national convention in Philadelphia, was winding things down in the same fashion that it had gaveled the session open: with a sense of unanimity and purpose. President William McKinley would of course be the presidential nominee of the state's delegates, and it was further agreed that Minnesota senator William Washburn would make a fine, favorite-son candidate for vice president.

All that remained for the convention to do was choose alternate delegates for the trip to Philly. These seats were largely ceremonial, but they held a great deal of symbolic importance to at least one constituency in the hall: its small contingent of African American delegates. When a member of this group, J. Frank Wheaton, took the floor to speak to the convention, "hardly anybody but Wheaton knew what he was going to do." But according to the *Minneapolis Times*, he would soon "hypnotize the convention with oratory."

Wheaton began his talk by reminding the convention that its members belonged to the party of Lincoln, and, as such, they ought to remember their roots. Democrats were trying to win black votes by claiming that the United States was "waging an unholy war against the colored people of the Philippines," Wheaton said, and they were making headway with this argument. The GOP couldn't afford to ignore its core constituents, and one of the surest ways for Minnesota Republicans to maintain that support was to nominate an African American as a delegate to the national convention. Wheaton knew just who that man ought to be.

"Before the delegates had time to pull up the lower jaws [at Wheaton's impassioned speech] they dropped in amazement when they heard him

The campus's Pattee Hall law building (at left), photographed by Sweet about 1895

nominate himself," the *Minneapolis Journal* wrote the next day. The huzzahs and whoop-de-do were general. The assembly had yet to calm itself when the chairman put Wheaton's nomination to a vote. "Before the convention scarce knew what had happened, Mr. Wheaton had won the prize."

It wasn't the first time Frank Wheaton had dropped jaws and won prizes in the political arena of Minnesota. From the moment he landed in the state in 1893, Wheaton had distinguished himself in both the black and the white communities of the Twin Cities. He was, by all accounts, a gifted orator and a vibrant figure, who by sheer dint of personality rose to prominence in state Republican circles, only to walk away from the limelight as quickly as he had entered it.

Frank Wheaton was the first African American to graduate from the University of Minnesota's Law School (in 1894), and he was elected class orator. He twice represented the state's Republicans at national political conventions, and, in 1898, Wheaton was the first African American to be elected to the state legislature, where he represented the Kenwood district of Minneapolis. It was estimated that only about one hundred of Kenwood's forty thousand constituents were African Americans, and yet Frank Wheaton won his race in a veritable cakewalk. There wouldn't be another black legislator in the state of Minnesota for more than seventy years.

J. Frank Wheaton, the first African American to graduate from the university's Law School and the first African American state legislator

What made Wheaton's ascendancy even more remarkable was the fact that it ran counter to national trends. With the collapse of Reconstruction and the advent of Jim Crow laws, African American political power was on the wane in the 1890s. Just how John Francis Wheaton bucked the odds and became, as he was designated in a political biography of the day, one of "The Progressive Men of Minnesota" is one of the many small mysteries that surround his life's story.

Born in Maryland in 1866, Wheaton arrived in Minneapolis with political laurels already won in his native state. There he had been named as a delegate to state Republican conventions in 1887, 1889, and 1891, and, when he was all of twenty-two years of age, in 1888, he had attended the Republican national convention for the first time, as an alternate delegate from Maryland. He studied law with an attorney in his hometown of Hagerstown and then went off to Washington, D.C., where he attended the law school at Howard University and worked as a clerk in the U.S. Congress. After passing the bar in Maryland in 1892, he decided to pull up stakes and move to Minnesota.

We can only speculate on why he chose to come west to join the small community of African Americans living in Minnesota at the time. He may have visited Minneapolis during the 1892 Republican National Convention and liked what he saw. He may have been encouraged by the University of Minnesota's first African American graduate, Andrew Hilyer, who had also studied law at Howard University and was a familiar and powerful figure in Washington's African American community. Wheaton may have simply thrown a dart at a map on a wall.

After his stint at the University law school and now planted in Minnesota, Wheaton took a job as a clerk in the state legislature and then as a deputy clerk in the municipal court system of the city of Minneapolis. He also had a private law practice and became a pillar of the local African American community, where, among other good works, he spearheaded efforts in the legislature to pass civil rights legislation. This 1899 statute broadened and strengthened an already existing Minnesota law, which granted equal access for all races to a long list of public places and conveyances, including inns, taverns, public transportation, and dining establishments.

Exactly what prompted Wheaton to leave Minnesota and the legislature remains uncertain, but it is known that even before the 1900 state Republican convention, he had taken a job with an insurance company in Chicago. As a consequence, his business and political life in Minnesota was probably coming to an end before he took the floor that May. His appearance as an alternate delegate at the national convention in Philadelphia turned out to be Frank Wheaton's swan song, not simply in the state of Minnesota but also in the Republican Party.

He left with a salute to his adopted city and the suggestion that he might someday return: "I am not going to forswear my allegiance to Minneapolis, which I love better than any place on earth," he told a reporter from the *Minneapolis Times* in December 1899, soon after taking his new job, "and I will get back here every time I get a chance. I got my start here and I owe a great deal to the people of this city, where everyone is accorded 'equal rights' without regard to race, color or previous condition of servitude."

By 1905, Wheaton had opened a law practice in Manhattan and was once again in the headlines, this time representing African American victims of a race riot. The practice, opened with another African American attorney who had spent time as a lawyer in Minnesota, James Curtis, would become one of the most successful black firms in the city. At about the same time, Wheaton joined the Democratic Party in New York—we can only guess at the cause of this shift—and became a prominent member of the city's black caucus. He ran for the New York State Assembly from a Manhattan district in 1919, and, although he was defeated, Wheaton was given a position in the city district attorney's office.

Frank Wheaton was long a member of the Black Elks Club—a vital component of the African American community—and became that organization's national president in 1912. As a distinguished citizen of the burgeoning Harlem community, he rubbed elbows with a host of African American celebrities and served as an adviser to heavyweight boxing champion Jack Johnson; as a community organizer with the famed Vaudeville entertainer Bert Williams; and as counsel for the first wife of Marcus Garvey in a contentious and well-publicized divorce proceeding.

Wheaton's life came to a tragic and abrupt end in January 1922. The previous fall he had stood bail for a client, who had subsequently skipped, leaving

Wheaton holding a $10,000 bond. According to articles in New York papers, friends and colleagues helped Wheaton search all through the nooks and crannies of Harlem for the runaway client, but they failed to find the man. Despondent and faced with financial ruin because of the debt, Wheaton took his own life by inhaling gas on January 15, 1922.

Minnesota's first African American legislator, J. Frank Wheaton, was buried in Woodlawn Cemetery in the Bronx, New York, after a funeral procession through the streets of Harlem. A reported twenty thousand people lined Lenox and Seventh Avenues to pay their respects to the man, and it took a full three limousines to transport all the floral bouquets from his funeral to the gravesite.

In the Twin Cities, Wheaton's death was noted by several papers, including the *Minneapolis Journal*, which remembered "the audacity and cleverness" of his 1900 speech at the state Republican convention and saluted "the spectacular career of J. Frank Wheaton, Negro lawyer."

The Law School's class of 1894, with Wheaton barely visible in the back row (behind first-row man wearing light-colored pants)

Roy Wilkins (center) with Martin Luther King Jr. (left) and future Supreme Court justice Thurgood Marshall (right), 1959
(photo by Cecil Layne)

Remembering Roy Wilkins

IN APRIL 1955, University of Minnesota graduate Roy Wilkins (B.A. '23) became the leader of the oldest, best-organized, and—to use Wilkins's own adjective—"wiliest" civil rights group in the country: the National Association for the Advancement of Colored People. For the next twenty-two years, Wilkins led the NAACP through the most tumultuous and dramatic years of the civil rights movement and, in the process, became one of the best-known and most highly respected leaders of the struggle in the United States.

Though clearly a giant in the movement, Roy Wilkins was not universally admired. His years in office were contentious times, and the spectrum of thought within the African American community on how best to achieve political equality and social justice was wide. Militants like H. Rap Brown and Stokely Carmichael felt Wilkins and the NAACP moved far too slowly, and Wilkins, the supreme advocate of integration, viewed the Black Power Movement as pushing for a sort of reverse form of segregation.

Wilkins and the Reverend Martin Luther King Jr. were more often allies than at odds, but they were not the best of friends. Wilkins was rational and cool, a man who thought the best tools available in building change were diligence, persistence, and organization. He mistrusted leaders who used their positions to rouse emotions that were quickly dissipated.

"As anyone close to Wilkins during the 22 years he led the NAACP can attest," wrote Gilbert Jonas, a longtime colleague at that organization, "his patience with men of the cloth often wore thin. His own soft-spoken, erudite style of speaking was (perhaps deliberately) in utter contrast to the garrulous, gesticulating, rhythmic, and often fever-pitched style of Negro ministers, particularly those of the Baptist and evangelical denominations. His approach to ideas was persistently analytic, requiring evidence and proof to make a point. In his thinking, there was no room for an argument that rested on faith alone."

In his home state of Minnesota, Wilkins's life and times were shamefully neglected for many years. Despite his being a figure of national renown and importance, there was little attempt to claim him as a Minnesotan until late in his career. He was born in Mississippi and spent the first few years of his life in St. Louis, but Roy Wilkins grew up near Rice Street in St. Paul in a neighborhood "full of Swedes and Germans, French, Irish, and Jews," according to his autobiography, *Standing Fast*. Wilkins was five years old when his mother died of tuberculosis and he came to St. Paul, along with his brother, Earl, and his sister, Armeda, to be raised by an aunt and an uncle.

According to Wilkins, his was, for the most part, a pleasant childhood in a loving family, though not without its trials. His uncle, Sam Williams, worked for the Northern Pacific Railroad, managing the personal railroad car for the company president. The family was far from wealthy but did not lack any of the basic necessities. Wilkins stayed close to his own "quiet neighborhood" and away from "the turf belonging to the Rice Street Gang, the toughest kids in the city," where "the word 'nigger' was part of the equipment, along with other brickbats." Despite these constraints, Wilkins would later say that it was in St. Paul that he first learned it was not impossible "for white people and black people to live next door to one another, to get along—even to love one another."

Wilkins went to Whittier Grammar School, where he was the only African American in his class, but he felt comfortable with the working-class backgrounds of his fellow students. He was a fine student and was asked each year to recite the Gettysburg Address, though, he later wrote: "I see now that they picked me because I was a Negro; at the time I thought rather vainly that it was because I was the best reader in the class."

From Whittier, Wilkins matriculated to Mechanical Arts High School, where he expressed an early interest in engineering as a career. As a junior, however, he was chosen over two white students to be editor of the school's literary magazine, a distinction that won him a mention in the *Crisis*, the magazine of the NAACP, published in New York and edited by the famed W. E. B. DuBois. This item in a national publication was enough to make his interest in writing seem more glamorous than his interest in engineering. By the time Wilkins graduated from Mechanical Arts as class salutatorian in 1919, the focus of his studies had shifted to journalism, and he entered the University of Minnesota intent on pursuing a career in that field.

Wilkins wrote many years after the fact that he "was not a big man on campus." For that, you needed to live on Fraternity Row near the university, and black students were simply not allowed there. But according to an

F. Inge H. Inge Butler Richardson King Wilkins Harris T. Inge Kyle

article published in the *St. Paul Pioneer Press* in 1970, fellow African American students in his day considered Wilkins a leader of a group that numbered between fifteen and twenty-five students. A fellow student from St. Paul, Lafeyette Fields, is quoted as saying, "He was very influential and always willing to help. . . . [Wilkins] spearheaded a series of student-led community forums at the Hallie Q. Brown House," a center that encouraged young people in the community to attend college.

When he and his Omega Psi Phi frat brothers found themselves pictured in the 1923 *Gopher* annual, looking, according to Wilkins, "like a crew of hopeful bankers," they had the distinction of being the first African American organization to ever appear in the yearbook.

Wilkins broke more ground at the university. During his second year of college, he became the first black student to become a reporter for the *Minnesota Daily*, the student-run newspaper, though his "exhilaration at the breakthrough was deflated somewhat when I picked up the paper and saw that the editors had listed me on the masthead as Ray Wilkins." Nonetheless, he worked at the newspaper through his remaining years in college and picked up another honor in the spring of 1922 when he won third place in the school's prestigious annual Pillsbury Oratorical Contest.

For all his triumphs and accomplishments, Wilkins also found the moment in which he "lost [his] innocence on race once and for all." It happened in the summer of 1920, when a mob in Duluth, Minnesota, lynched three African American circus workers. Any sense that Minnesota was a place peculiarly blessed by racial tolerance vanished in the brutality of that dark night.

"I was just short of nineteen the night that the bodies of [Isaac] McGhie, [Elmer] Jackson, and [Elias] Clayton swung from a light pole in Duluth," Wilkins would write almost sixty years later. "I read the stories in the newspapers and put them down feeling sick, scared, and angry all at the same time. This was Minnesota, not Mississippi, but every Negro in the John Robinson

Roy Wilkins debated James Kilpatrick on campus amid protests over the visit of Alabama's governor George Wallace. *(Minnesota Daily, February 17, 1964)*

Show had been suspect in the eyes of the police and guilty in the eyes of the mob. . . . I found myself thinking of black people as a very vulnerable us—and white people as an unpredictable, violent them."

After his graduation in 1923, Wilkins would spend just one more year in the Twin Cities, serving as editor for the long-standing local black newspaper, the *Appeal*. When he was offered a higher-paying job at a newspaper in Kansas City, he took it and moved into the wider realm of the nation's African American community. Walter White, whom Wilkins would ultimately succeed as executive secretary of the NAACP, asked Wilkins to come work for the organization in New York in 1931. Three years later, he was named acting editor of the *Crisis*, succeeding DuBois. It was the very journal that had launched Wilkins on his career in journalism, and he would stay in the post for the next fifteen years.

When White died of a heart attack in March 1955, Wilkins stepped into the leadership role at the NAACP. He would see it through the next two decades of triumph, tragedy, and struggle, including the 1963 March on Washington, at which Wilkins spoke; the assassination of Dr. King; and, perhaps most notably for the NAACP, the passage of the 1964 Civil Rights

Act, the single most important piece of civil rights legislation enacted in the twentieth century.

Meanwhile, Wilkins's legacy in Minnesota and at the university was undervalued and little acknowledged through most of his stellar career. One searches in vain through local media archives during the early years of his tenure at the NAACP for stories describing the successes of this son of Minnesota. Even when Wilkins was at the height of his influence and fame, a leading figure in the fight for passage of the Civil Rights Act, he came back to the campus with a stunning lack of recognition. In February 1964, Wilkins arrived at Northrop Auditorium to debate the merits of the act with James J. Kilpatrick, who would go on to fame in the 1970s as one of the Point-Counterpoint debaters on *60 Minutes.* The next day's coverage of the event in both the *Minnesota Daily* and the *Minneapolis Star* fails to even mention the fact that Wilkins was a proud Minnesotan and a graduate of the state's university.

In time, there would be some rectification for oversights like these. In the 1970s, Wilkins was awarded an honorary degree from the University of Minnesota Graduate School. Three years after his death in 1981, the city of St. Paul named the auditorium adjoining its Civic Center (now the Xcel Energy Center) in Roy Wilkins's honor. In 1992, the university endowed a $2 million chair and the Center for Human Relations and Social Justice at the Humphrey Institute in Wilkins's name. And in 1996, the university built Wilkins Hall, a student residence, on the East Bank campus.

Wilkins's peerless work in the struggle for civil rights deserves as much and more. In a ceremony honoring Wilkins soon after his retirement, President Jimmy Carter said to him, "You have helped to write history." And Ramsey Clark, former U.S. attorney general, said that Wilkins was "a man of gentleness and integrity who enriched all our lives with justice." Upon Wilkins's death, the Reverend Jesse Jackson called him "a man of integrity, intelligence and courage who, with his broad shoulders, bore more than his share of responsibility for our and the nation's advancement."

Gate 27 in Memorial Stadium, doorway to the Laboratory of Physiological Hygiene until the stadium was demolished in 1991 (1953 photograph)

Behind Gate 27

N March 16, 1937, University of Minnesota president Lotus Coffman began a slightly worried letter to the dean of the Medical School, Harold Diehl (M.D. '17):

My dear Dr. Diehl,

Mr. Frank G. McCormick [the athletic director at the U] called on me yesterday to discuss a problem relative to the teaching of anatomy and physiology to students in physical education. He states that for a number of years this instruction was given by a member of the staff of the Department of Anatomy. Later it was taken over by Dr. Cooke. Now that Dr. Cooke has retired, there is no one in the Department of Physical Education for Men competent to give this instruction. . . . The result is that Mr. McCormick has been searching for someone else to do the work.

This may sound like a dry note in the long history of University of Minnesota faculty appointments, but it foretells the beginning of one of the most distinguished medical science careers ever at the university. It also signals the start of a world-renowned institution in Minnesota and informs a curious footnote in campus history.

The distinguished career belongs to Dr. Ancel Keys, who remains one of the giants of Minnesota science. The institution that he founded, initially called the Laboratory of Physiological Hygiene (LPH), has evolved into the Division of Epidemiology within the School of Public Health. The curious footnote is the fact that for fifty years, first as the Laboratory of Physiological Hygiene and then as "Epi," this unit conceived and conducted some of medical science's most important and pioneering studies in cardiovascular health from quarters beneath the bleachers of a Big Ten football stadium. A warren of lab rooms and offices behind Gate 27, near the visitors' locker room on the south side of Memorial Stadium, was the unlikely home of groundbreaking scientific research, from World War II until the structure was torn down in 1991.

The force behind those studies—the man who would ultimately be hired to give those lectures in physiology—was born in 1904 in Colorado Springs, Colorado, and died in Minneapolis in 2004, at the age of one hundred. In 2000, the *St. Paul Pioneer Press* named Ancel Keys as one of the ten most influential scientists in the state's history, as well as one of its 150 most distinguished citizens. But when Lotus Coffman wrote his March 1937 letter to Harold Diehl, fame was a long way off for Ancel Keys. He was not yet at the university, the Laboratory of Physiological Hygiene had not yet been created, and Gate 27 was just another means to get to a Saturday afternoon Gophers game.

Coffman was hoping that Diehl could find someone from the Medical School's Department of Physiology to lecture Frank McCormick's physical education students. There was nothing momentous about the request, but the fact that Coffman was involved suggests that some interdepartmental niceties needed to be observed. "It seems to me," he wrote to Diehl, "that it would be a mistake to have persons teaching physiology to students in physical education who have no connection with the Department of Physiology."

At the time, physical education for men and the athletics department were a combined unit, headed by McCormick. Physical education as a pursuit and study was about forty years old on the campus. Its first director was another legendary figure at the university: Dr. Louis Cooke, the same Dr. Cooke whose lectures would ultimately be taken over by Ancel Keys.

"Doc" Cooke, as he was universally known, had arrived in 1897, armed with a medical degree from the University of Vermont and experience running YMCA programs in Toledo, Ohio, and Minneapolis. In addition to his studies at Vermont, Cooke had spent time in the 1890s at the YMCA's famed training facility in Springfield, Massachusetts—at about the same time as and at the same institution where another doctor, James Naismith, was inventing basketball. Perhaps not surprisingly, Doc Cooke brought the game to the University of Minnesota and served as the basketball team's head coach into the 1920s.

Physical education as a concept was a product of the nineteenth century, and the YMCA—along with a variety of other movements, most notably, the Turner gymnastic clubs, which had been brought to this country by German immigrants—was a leader in promoting the notion of physical exercise as a social, cultural, and moral good. The industrial revolution and an ever-increasing urban population were thought to be promoting a kind

of flabbiness, both literal and figurative, in the body politic. Physical education was considered therapeutic, not just for sagging muscles, but for sagging minds and manners, as well.

Studies at the time searched for direct scientific correlations between "ideal" body types and "ideal" brains, and Doc Cooke conducted his own anthropometric studies along these lines. Within the University Archives today, in Doc Cooke's papers, are long, carefully noted lists of students named, noted by academic ability, and measured for height, weight, and ability to lift weights.

Health and science were considered a part of physical education from its earliest days, and pioneer directors of university phys-ed programs across the country tended to be medical doctors and students of physiology. This was true at the University of Minnesota too. Aside from Doc Cooke, notable leaders in physical education J. Anna Norris, who headed the Department of Physical Education for Women, and Henry Williams, the football coach, were also M.D.s.

"Doc" Cooke (foreground) in the physical education and athletics office (with the Little Brown Jug trophy hanging from the ceiling), 1905

After the turn of the century, there came a philosophic backlash against the overly serious mission given physical education in its infancy. Reformers felt that the simple play involved in physical activity was its chief therapeutic value and that play served its own social function. This sense of fun was echoed by what was happening on campuses throughout the country. During the 1910s and 1920s, intramural sports boomed, as did the power and influence of intercollegiate athletics.

The scientific and health-oriented missions of physical education — including physiological hygiene — were not diminished by this new sensibility, but the many purposes of physical activity and physical education and the needs of student hygiene at the university were lumped together. J. Anna Norris, for instance, served as a health officer for university women, doing physicals and examining student lodging for sanitation purposes — along with serving as head of the women's Physical Education Department.

As a consequence, the Department of Physical Education and Athletics became a sprawling concern, and issues regarding the definitions and management of physical education were still being worked out late in the 1930s — which is one of the reasons Frank McCormick asked for President Coffman's help in finding someone to teach anatomy and physiology to his students. Coffman called upon Dean Diehl because it seemed sensible to him to have that someone come from the Medical School. Diehl organized a meeting to address Coffman's letter. Attending, besides Diehl, were Frank McCormick, his assistant athletic director Louis Keller, Dr. C. M. Jackson of the Medical School's Department of Anatomy, and Dr. Maurice Visscher, the newly appointed head of the Department of Physiology (and another future giant in the history of University of Minnesota medicine). The letter they sent back to Coffman on April 27 has no ifs, ands, or buts about it:

> There was complete agreement upon the most desirable course of procedure. . . . We should have [a lecturer] connected jointly with these departments of the Medical School who is soundly trained in anatomy and physiology, has an interest in their applications to physical education and has a definite interest in and capacity for investigative work in these fields. . . . Mr. McCormick and Mr. Keller both feel that it would be preferable to have such a person associated with these scientific departments of the Medical School rather than more or less scientifically isolated in the Department of Physical Education. Mr. McCormick stated that the Department of Physical Education and Athletics will be glad to contribute as much as seems proper toward the salary and research activity of such a person.

In 1937, Ancel Keys was spending an unsatisfying year at the Mayo Clinic, alleviated by the fact that he met his wife, Margaret, while working there.

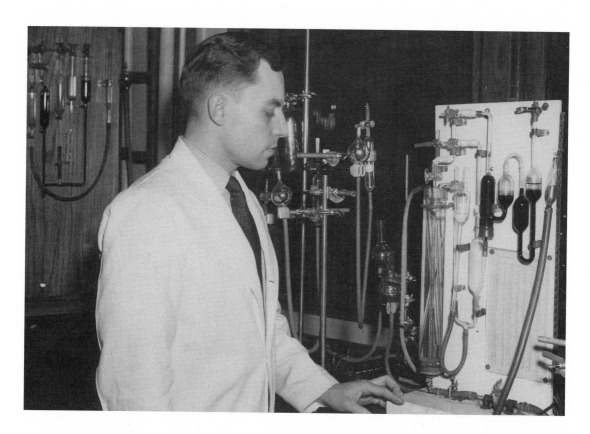

He had arrived in Minnesota from the Harvard faculty, where he had held a low-level position in that college's Fatigue Laboratory. The Mayo Clinic had promised a higher salary and a more prestigious post, but life in Rochester turned out to be a little staid for Keys.

Born in Colorado, Keys had grown up in the Bay Area of California and had had an adventure-filled youth, which included surviving the great 1906 earthquake and fire that devastated San Francisco. After the quake, Keys's family moved briefly to Los Angeles, where they stayed for a time with Keys's uncle, the actor Lon Chaney. Then it was back north to Berkeley, where Keys spent most of his childhood and wound up attending the University of California. There he earned a bachelor's degree in economics after only two years of study. A postgraduate job painting furniture for Woolworth's convinced him that his future lay in other pursuits. Back at Berkeley, and on the advice of a famed professor of zoology, Charles Atwood Kofoid, he decided to study biology.

Keys got his master's degree in six months and his Ph.D. just two years after that. In 1930, he won a fellowship from the National Research Council to study with a Nobel laureate in physiology from Copenhagen, Dr. August Krogh. There he did research on the physiology of eels, specifically on the

Researcher Ancel Keys in his laboratory, about 1938. At the army's request he developed "K rations" for use during World War II.

"eel problem," as Dr. Krogh called it: How can eels survive in both freshwater and saltwater? (He found the answer in their gills, which were able to regulate the levels of sodium in their blood.)

Keys's dizzying ascent in the world of science continued. In 1931, a Rockefeller Foundation Fellowship took him to Cambridge University in England, where he was awarded another Ph.D., from King's College. At Harvard, he joined the Fatigue Laboratory (where research was concerned with physiological adaptations of humans to adverse environmental conditions) and became interested in the physiological and biochemical effects of high altitudes on the human body. He led a team to the Andes, climbed to twenty thousand feet, and spent ten days at that height studying its effects on his body's ability to function.

Friday night bridge parties in Rochester, a year later, seemed a long way down the slope for Ancel Keys. He finished his report on his studies in the Andes at Mayo and did further physiological research, but at the end of the year he was more than happy to entertain an offer to do research and teach at the University of Minnesota.

Keys arrived on campus in 1937 and was given an office at Millard Hall. His duties, aside from teaching "physiology and the physiology of exercise courses to physical education students," included "direct research in physical education with emphasis on the physiology of exercise." And it was understood that his little room was inadequate and that space would be found eventually for a laboratory. Keys reported to Maurice Visscher in the Medical School, but his salary and the funds for equipment and assistants for his research came from athletic department receipts. A little more space was found for Keys within Millard Hall, and he dubbed the area the Laboratory of Physiological Hygiene after a similarly named laboratory at Harvard. Keys began research on the physical differences between athletes and non-athletes at the university, looking specifically at comparisons of heart sizes and functions.

But these studies were put on hold when, in 1940, Keys got his first request from the War Department. War had broken out in Europe, and it was looming for the United States. Would Dr. Keys be willing to devise a nutritious ration for army paratroopers? "I went down to a local grocery store," says Keys, "picked up some food that I thought might be good and nutritious and took them back to the lab." The first K rations, named for Keys, were tested by soldiers at Fort Snelling soon after. More extensive studies were done a few months later with paratroopers at Fort Benning, Georgia. The army was so impressed with the results that the rations ultimately became standard field issue to all GIs through the duration of the war.

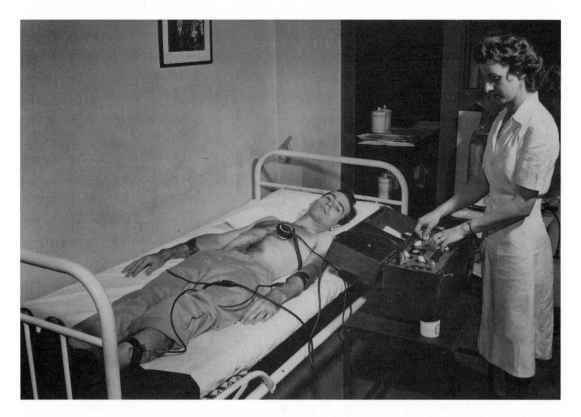

The initial success prompted requests from the army for more studies, and Keys needed space to carry these out. Frank McCormick found some, beneath the south tower of Memorial Stadium, and in the summer of 1942, the LPH moved behind Gate 27. In its early days, the laboratory consisted of about eleven thousand square feet, with office space, five chemistry and physical measurement laboratories, four "special experiment" rooms, an X-ray room, and a metabolism room. Dormitories for the thirty-six subjects of the laboratory's starvation studies (conscientious objectors volunteered to undergo food deprivation) were added later in the war. Photos from a brochure created by LPH to describe those experiments give a sense of what was behind Gate 27 during the war. They show treadmills the size of Buicks, and subjects chugging along on their revolving belts. Lab-coated scientists hold stopwatches beside them.

The starvation study, which came on the heels of Keys's and the laboratory's work on nutrition for the army, pushed LPH further from its initial responsibilities to the Physical Education Department. At the beginning of the nutritional work, it was understood, by both the dean of the Medical School and the director of the Department of Physical Education and Athletics that Keys's initial responsibilities, "to direct research in physical education" and teach physiology to phys-ed students, would resume after the war.

A wartime conscientious objector being monitored during a starvation experiment at the Laboratory of Physiological Hygiene, 1944

Conscientious
objectors eating
dinner while
participating in
Keys's starvation
experiments, 1944

As a consequence, Physical Education and Athletics continued to provide funds for the laboratory.

By 1946, however, it had become obvious that LPH had morphed into something that belonged outside the Department of Physical Education and Athletics. Keys also wanted to escape the oversight of the Medical School. That year, he asked that LPH be transferred into the School of Public Health. "The current work of the Laboratory of Physiological Hygiene," read the request to the president, "is geared almost exclusively for experimental research in the field of biochemistry as it relates to normal human activities. The commitments of this laboratory are such . . . that it is very difficult to service the students in physical education and to meet their needs as is demanded in a modern program of physical education."

And so it was. The LPH moved into the School of Public Health, and Keys's interests shifted toward the study of cholesterol and its effects on the human heart. Renown would come to him and LPH through the next twenty-five years of research, beginning with the starvation study, which would become world famous, filling in a large blank in the scientific literature by describing the most effective way to rehabilitate a semi-starved population. The results of the study, published in two thick volumes in 1950 as

Biology of Human Starvation, remain a seminal description of human physiological and psychological responses to starvation.

Keys's high profile continued, as he became one of the first medical scientists to examine and describe the relationship between cholesterol and heart disease. He and others at the laboratory pioneered the study of cardiovascular epidemiology, most notably through a famed research project that became known as the Seven Countries Study. In it, Keys and his colleagues examined populations in seven locales around the globe, comparing the frequency of cardiovascular disease in cultural context. Their research was the first to note rates of heart attack and stroke in contrasting cultures with varying diets and, in the words of Keys's colleague Dr. Henry Blackburn (M.S. '57), "led many in the field of health to think in terms of 'sick and well populations' as well as sick and well individuals."

In January 1961, *Time* magazine put Dr. Ancel Keys on its cover to salute his work on the link between diet and heart disease, as well as his past contributions to physiology. Eleven years later, Keys retired from LPH, replaced by Blackburn, an LPH veteran, who organized a merger between the laboratory and the School of Medicine's Division of Epidemiology.

Meanwhile, as Keys and his colleagues in the laboratory traveled to distant parts of the globe studying heart disease and its causes, scientists would in turn visit Gate 27, wondering why such important scientific study was being conducted beneath a football stadium.

Epi eventually grew out of its quarters in Memorial Stadium, and the stadium itself was torn down. Blackburn led the Division of Epidemiology into the modern era by expanding and diversifying its interests and establishing a series of ongoing community studies and programs that both studied epidemiological problems and promoted interventions in health problems. The many research and public health programs of the division would continue in fine new quarters, and Epi would continue to expand its good works—all arising from the university's need to find someone to take Doc Cooke's place lecturing physical education students.

Novelist Robert Penn Warren in his university office, 1949

King Red

O N JANUARY 19, 1950, floodlights swept the skies of downtown Minneapolis above the Orpheum Theater on Hennepin and Ninth, calling moviegoers to the local premier of a film that, were it not for the presence of Robert Penn Warren, probably wouldn't have had much more local appeal than the other big opener that weekend, *Father Was a Fullback,* starring Fred MacMurray. Sure, *All the King's Men* had debuted nationally in New York in November to stellar reviews; but its subject matter—the rise and fall of a southern politician whose life looked an awfully lot like that of former Louisiana governor Huey Long—was far more likely to cause a stir in Baton Rouge than in Minneapolis. Then again, here was the story's author, Mr. Warren, shaking hands at the Orpheum with a few hundred of his friends, fans, family members, and colleagues from the University of Minnesota, where Warren taught in the English Department.

Warren's novel *All the King's Men* had been published to rave reviews in the fall of 1946, and a year later, it was awarded the Pulitzer Prize for Fiction. The movie would turn out to be a faithful version of Warren's story—one that the author not only applauded but helped write. It would reap awards, garnering a Best Picture statue from the Academy in 1949, as well as an Oscar for lead actor Broderick Crawford and a Best Supporting Actress nod to Mercedes McCambridge.

Robert Penn Warren had created one of the most enduring stories in all of American literature. In Willie Stark, the fatally flawed politician, who sells his soul for the love and votes of "the people," Warren made a lasting portrait of good political intentions gone bad. The supporting cast of characters, including a cynical foil to Stark named Jack Burden, and the woman they both love, Anne Stanton, are pretty effective, too.

As memorable as the characters in the novel is the world from which they came. Warren paints a sharp image of barefoot poverty mixed with cynical privilege — of dusty country roads and sweat-stained politicos in suspenders, fanning themselves with straw hats as they lean against a circle of pickup trucks and listen to the rabble-rousing orations of Willie Stark. It feels so quintessentially southern, circa 1932, that few will recall that the bulk of this bayou-based story was written in a land of snow and ice.

Warren arrived on the campus of the University of Minnesota in the fall of 1942, with a solid reputation in the literary world but not much renown beyond the pipe-smoking, tweed-coated sanctums of prewar English department faculties. Born in 1905 and raised in western Kentucky, Warren graduated from Vanderbilt University and then earned a master's degree from the University of California. He went to Oxford as a Rhodes scholar in 1930 and started his first teaching job at Southwestern College in Memphis. Warren began publishing poetry, taught briefly at Vanderbilt and the University of Iowa, and wrote a biography of John Brown, which had begun as his thesis at Oxford.

Meanwhile, Louisiana's recently elected governor, Huey P. Long, was attempting to boost the academic standing of his state's largest college by recruiting better faculty. It was on the wave of this reform that Warren was hired at Louisiana State University in 1934.

Aside from observing the career of Huey Long in Baton Rouge (though the two never met), Warren built his literary reputation there, first as a poet, then as a scholar, then as editor of a widely respected journal, the *Southern Review*, founded by him and a colleague at LSU named Cleanth Brooks. Brooks and Warren also collaborated on two college texts, *Understanding Poetry* and *Understanding Fiction*, which became instant classics, hailed for their modernist views of interpreting literature.

LSU, however, was not so interested in maintaining its budding literary reputation. First the *Southern Review* was killed for lack of funds, and then an anticipated $200 salary increase was yanked away from Warren. Coincidental to this neglect, the LSU football team received $2,500 for a new cage for its mascot, a Bengal tiger.

There happened to be an offer from the recently appointed chair of the University of Minnesota's English Department, a man named Joseph Warren Beach, sitting on Warren's desk as all of this transpired. It was for $4,000 per year, the same amount that LSU had been about to give Warren before it set aside $2,500 for the tiger's cage. Despite some misgivings about heading away from his southern roots, Warren decided it was time to leave Baton Rouge.

He arrived in Minnesota in the fall of 1942 and was immediately happy to be working for and with Joseph Beach. Beach was the nephew of former university president Cyrus Northrop and had been around the campus since his freshman year in 1896. Despite his status as a graybeard, Beach was a modernist, who had made his scholarly reputation by publishing a book called *The Method of Henry James*, which, according to a later reviewer, "broke the ground for what is now called 'the new or analytical' criticism of literature."

Beach had admirers among many of the young literary critics of the day, including Warren, Malcolm Cowley, and Allen Tate. Thus Warren was coming to one of the most highly regarded English faculties in the country; and as if to prove the point (and his own growing reputation), that year Beach paired "Red" Warren with 1930 Nobel laureate Sinclair "Red" Lewis to teach a special course in creative writing. Lewis came on board the faculty in the

Joseph W. Beach, who built up the English Department's highly regarded faculty, about 1940

first semester of 1942, and Warren continued Lewis's course through the spring of 1943.

No doubt the tag team of Reds made an intimidating combination for would-be young authors, but the quality of student writing at the time was outstanding. Among the young scribes learning the craft at the university in those years were Tom Heggen, who would soon write the best-selling World War II novel *Mr. Roberts* (which became a successful Broadway play and a prize-winning movie starring Henry Fonda and Jack Lemon); and St. Paul–born writer Max Shulman, who authored a very popular novel called *Barefoot Boy with Cheek* and followed that up by creating the characters Dobie Gillis and Maynard G. Krebs in *The Many Loves of Dobie Gillis*.

Warren socialized with both Heggen and Shulman and became especially friendly with the latter. The two would eventually share the same literary agent in New York (the high-powered Helen Strauss), and, according to one Warren scholar, they even collaborated on a movie treatment. The creator of Willie Stark and the creator of Maynard G. Krebs may seem like an unlikely team, but unlikely was the atmosphere at the University of Minnesota in the day. Add to the mix Saul Bellow, who joined the faculty as an instructor in 1946, and local authors like Meridel LeSueur, Frederick Manfred, and James Gray, and Dinkytown in the 1940s sounds a little bit like Greenwich Village, you betcha.

But Warren was clearly the star of the show. Even before the great success of *All the King's Men*, he had had impeccable credentials as a poet, critic, and budding novelist (his book *At Heaven's Gate* was published to high praise in 1944); and he was an outstanding teacher as well. A 1945 article in the *Daily* claimed that students were packed "like sardines" into his classes. "Since coming [to the U of M], Warren has been the idol of a growing cult of devotees," the story read. "Students say he makes them understand literature as they never had before. . . . Persons who meet him for the first time come away remembering not his honors and distinction, but a sympathetic listener who knows a great deal about human nature."

Warren was handsome (Brenda Ueland called him a "Leslie-Howardish-looking-man") and articulate, with a slight drawl and a gift for imitating a variety of dialects and accents. He could also recite long sections of the *Rime of the Ancient Mariner*. But it wasn't only the student body who found him attractive. Warren was drawing praise and promotions from the administration. He earned substantial salary bumps each year that he worked in Minneapolis, and the notes on his annual performance, passed between Beach and the dean of the College of Arts and Sciences, are steeped in expressions of his value to the school and department—"a brilliant teacher with an

enthusiastic following among students." "In the opinion of many competent judges Warren is our most distinguished living man of letters."

After the publication of *All the King's Men* and its subsequent fame and awards, Warren's star shone even brighter. He was now a figure of national repute, and a headline in the *Minneapolis Tribune* suggests a hint of the local expectations for the university's Pulitzer-winning author. "Warren Wins Prize, Keeps on Teaching," it read, as if it were a surprise that he bothered to show up, once again, in the classroom in the spring of 1947.

In fact, Robert Penn Warren did seem destined for a larger world, and he was drawn to New York in the fall of that year to help create a stage version of *All the King's Men*. He would be gone through the course of the year, working on a new novel and then the movie. Warren had received offers from a number of schools even before *All the King's Men* was published. Still, he liked the University of Minnesota, liked teaching, liked Joseph Beach, and

Robert Penn Warren
teaching a class,
about 1948

liked that he was appreciated in Minnesota, where, in addition to the annual raises, he was given two sabbaticals during his nine years at the school. Despite numerous offers, he stayed at the U of M until the spring of 1951, when a disintegrating marriage and the lure of a life closer to the literary and publishing establishments of New York led him to take a post at Yale University.

Robert Penn Warren remained near the forefront of American letters through the remainder of his career, which ultimately spanned sixty distinguished years of writing poetry, history, literary criticism, and novels. By the time he died in 1989, at the age of eighty-four, he had accrued a vita that few writers have equaled. It included three Pulitzer Prizes (two for his poetry and one for his fiction), several Guggenheim Fellowships, and one of the earliest MacArthur "genius grants." To cap his illustrious career, Warren was named the first poet laureate of the United States in 1986.

The university theater's production of Warren's *All the King's Men*, 1949

Only a few local obituaries remembered that the author of *All the King's Men* had achieved his first wide fame in the frozen North. His stay here became mostly a footnote in his long life and career. It was never Warren's home in the way that the South had been, but it had its share of moments for him. As he wrote Joseph Beach after leaving the university, "Resigning from Minnesota cost me a considerable twinge. Nobody could have been treated more kindly than I have been treated there, and no one could be happier than I was in my departmental associations."

A 1981 poem called "Minneapolis Story" suggests that Warren carried his stay here in his memories for many years to come. It reads in part:

> Long years ago, in Minneapolis,
> Dark falling, snow falling to celebrate
>
> The manger-birth of a babe in that snowless latitude,
> Church bells vying with whack of snow-chains on
>
> Fenders, there I, down a side street,
> Head thrust into snow-swirl, strove toward Hennepin.

Issues of the Day

Maria Sanford, university professor and activist, about 1880 *(photo by W. H. Jacoby & Son)*

Farsighted Foresters

IN JANUARY 1900, University of Minnesota rhetoric professor Maria Sanford employed all of her professional skills in an editorial blast from the pages of the *Courant*, the official journal of the Minnesota Federation of Women's Clubs. Her subject was the future of a large tract of forested land in north central Minnesota, near the headwaters of the Mississippi River. Her style was imperative: "This is an urgent, an uncompromising note of warning to those who faithfully urge, at the last possible opportunity, the preservation of one body of the massive and extensive pine forests of Minnesota, free from the annihilating, destructive slash of the lumberman's ax," wrote Sanford. "State pride, health, recreation and the best interests of this generation and of posterity, all demand that this last opportunity shall not pass without the most favorable action for a permanent forest reservation in Minnesota."

What had Sanford, and others in the Federation of Women's Clubs, so upset was the distinct possibility that land in the region near Minnesota's Cass, Leech, and Winnibigoshish Lakes — called the Chippewa Forest — was about to be sold through a congressional provision known as the Nelson Act. The law, according to Sanford, would allow "millionaire lumbermen" to "saw down, chop off and drive out every pine tree the region contains." This work, said Sanford, was all set to begin: "Mills are in active operation at and near Cass lake, lumbering camps in that region are numerous, three railroads penetrate the forests there."

"In the name of humanity," she continued, "is it not possible for the American people to favorably determine the results of an occasion so fraught with inestimable benefits . . . by permanently preserving the last public white pine forest that exists in America!"

The sense of crisis apparent in Sanford's plea was felt by a growing body of Minnesotans at the turn of the twentieth century. Over the previous fifty years, Americans had witnessed the awesome leveling of the great pine forests of Michigan and Wisconsin. The once-boundless woodland resources of the Upper Midwest were now reduced by vast acres of cutover slash and stumpage. Minnesota's timber industry had been active for at least half a century and had been working at full throttle for about twenty-five of those years, but it had not quite reached its peak lumber production in 1900. Which meant there was still land for developers and preservationists to battle over.

Enter the Minnesota Federation of Women's Clubs. Although the protection and wise usage of the nation's forests was a growing concern for a variety of progressives across the country in the late 1890s, in Minnesota no single organization was more active in promoting scientific forestry and the nascent conservation movement than the state's Women's Clubs.

Founded in 1895, three years after the National Federation of Women's Clubs was formed, the Minnesota Federation of Women's Clubs was an immediately popular and influential group of women. Its membership drew from the educated middle and upper classes, and it included the wives of some of Minnesota's most prominent leaders. In contrast to the stereotype of fussy matrons in flowered hats that would come to characterize the organization in years to come, the early Minnesota Women's Clubs were generally progressive in their thinking and were quite capable of stirring up controversy. With leaders like Sanford and Margaret Evans, who was principal of Carleton College and the first president of the federation, the group was viewed by the popular press of the day as the "Brainy Women of Minnesota." As if to confirm that image, improving educational opportunities through better library systems and the kindergarten movement were two of the organization's seminal goals.

In accordance with Victorian notions of the proper place for women, club members were also deeply involved in issues that could be labeled public domesticity—matters of civic sanitation, health, and beauty. The Women's Clubs were among the first groups in the state to promote a more systematic means of garbage collection in the Twin Cities. Likewise, they were active in promoting public health through measures such as a tuberculin test on the milk sold in the cities by regional dairy farmers.

The clubs' interest in health and beauty helped chart their path toward forestry and conservation. The salubrious effect on lungs, heart, and head of a visit to a pristine natural setting was a well-established notion in the rapidly urbanizing America of the 1890s. The creation of parks and the promotion of outdoor activities like golf and bicycle riding were high on Women's Clubs' agendas. It was no great leap, then, for the clubs to get involved when it looked as though the forests near the headwaters of the Mississippi were

about to be opened for public usage. The land "is situated in a charming lake country, largely upon non-agricultural soil," wrote Florence Bramhall, who would come to head the federation's Forest Reserve Committee. It was "precious for beauty, for health-giving ozone, for influence on climate, breaking as it does the high winds sweeping down from the North and West."

The forest described by Bramhall, the Chippewa, had emerged among a collection of shallow, glacial depressions in the north central part of the state. These had evolved into a landscape of bogs, lakes, and wet meadows of sedge and wild rice. The uplands portion of the region was covered with giant hardwoods and great, dense stands of red and white pine. Rich in fish and game, the place had been home to a succession of people for thousands of years. The most recent of these were the Ojibwe, whose Leech Lake Reservation was at the heart of the forest.

In the 1890s, this Ojibwe land became temptingly available to development by means of the onerous Dawes Act. This late nineteenth-century legislation was the primary tool used to dismantle Indian tribes and force individual Native Americans onto Euro-American-style farms of eighty acres apiece. According to its provisions, any acreage beyond those individual allotments—a substantial portion of the reservation—could be made available for public sale. It was here, in the disposition of these Ojibwe lands, where the battle was joined between advocates of forest conservation and regional development.

Despite the implication of Sanford's rhetoric, it was not just "millionaire lumbermen" who coveted the forest. Business interests from Grand Rapids to Duluth were eager to see homesteaders and lumberjacks come streaming into the region. And because so much of the opposition to the development of the forest centered in the Twin Cities, people who lived in other parts of the state tended to see the battle as between those who favored regional economic advancement and city "meddlers" who wanted a "hunting playground" for "a few nabobs who have more money than brains."

Women attending the annual meeting of the Minnesota Federation of Women's Clubs, an important organization promoting conservation of forest resources, 1905

The playground notion was born in the first proposal put forward by the Women's Clubs and their allies, who included Christopher Columbus Andrews, the head of the state's newly created Forestry Board, and a wealthy sportsman from Chicago named John Cooper. They suggested that a four-million-acre national park be created in the area. To help promote the idea in Washington, Cooper bankrolled and organized a Great Northern Railroad excursion to Cass Lake for one hundred congressmen in October 1899.

Although the tour brought exposure to the region, the delegation was not impressed enough to do much toward advancing the park. Four million acres was an awfully dear chunk of prime timberland to take out of the marketplace. "Not one member of Congress from Minnesota up to this time stands sponsor for the national park," wrote Sanford in the *Courant*, just three months later. Not only that: "It is plausibly hinted in interested quarters that the Secretary of the Interior is to be legally forced to proceed with the sale of timber."

It was this turn of events that prompted Sanford's fiery rhetoric about "the destructive slash of the lumberman's ax." It also prompted an emergency lobbying effort by Sanford and Lydia Phillips Williams, who had succeeded Margaret Evans as president of the Minnesota Federation of Women's Clubs. In February 1900, the pair boarded the train for Washington with the full blessing of the *Minneapolis Journal*. "National forest stock went up several points in public confidence today as the result of the announcement that Mrs. Lydia Phillips Williams . . . and Professor Maria Sanford, of the University of Minnesota, are going to Washington to take personal charge of the interests of the project." Sanford spent the next couple of weeks, and Williams the next couple of months, bending the ear of the Minnesota congressional delegation in Washington. They were successful in forestalling the immediate sale of timber in the region, but the park idea remained a nonstarter.

Back in Minnesota, Florence Bramhall and the Women's Clubs Forestry Committee worked to find a solution to this impasse. With the counsel of the young superintendent of the University of Minnesota's Agricultural Experiment Station in Grand Rapids, Herman Haupt Chapman, the Women's Clubs were soon touting a compromise that substantially reduced the acreage to be set aside and added provisions for a rational cut of the timber in the Chippewa Forest, with plans for reforestation. Gone was the inflammatory idea that the region would become a park for Twin Cities "nabobs." Instead, what would be created was a forest reserve, practicing the latest in scientific forestry.

For the next year and a half, the Federation of Women's Clubs, led by Bramhall and the Forestry Committee, did the hard, slogging job of selling this new proposal to the people of Minnesota, its leaders, and, ultimately, the U.S. Congress, which had final say in the disposition of this federal land. Bramhall accepted invitations to address the State Forestry Association, the State Horticultural Association, and the State Agricultural Association, where she promoted the forest reserve idea. To further publicize the proposal, a special issue of the *Courant* was devoted entirely to Chippewa Forest matters and then, according to Bramhall, "was put into the hands of the business men of St. Paul and Minneapolis, of the state editors, and wherever it was necessary that the issues involved should be clearly understood."

The lobbying worked. Pressure from state leaders created momentum within Minnesota's congressional delegation to, in Bramhall's words, "arrive at some decision." A December 1901 trip to Washington by Chapman helped further the plans at the capitol. Then a final blessing came from Gifford Pinchot, the head of the newly created National Forest Bureau and friend of President Theodore Roosevelt. Minnesota congressman Paige Morris introduced legislation creating a 225,000-acre forest reserve out of the lands taken from the Ojibwe reservation, and, in June 1902, President Roosevelt signed into law the means of creating the first congressionally mandated national forest in the country's history.

From a modern perspective, the provisions of the Morris Bill seem hardly a great conservation victory. Indeed, the fact that Duluth and Grand Rapids development interests went away happy suggests that compromise came at a price to the forest. A full 95 percent of the timber was made available for logging (this provision would be amended to 90 percent in a few years' time). Agricultural lands in the region were opened to settlement. Just 5 percent of the full-grown forest was set aside as beauty strips along lakeshores and for reforestation purposes. And of course this whole great debate was conducted at the expense of the Ojibwe people, who were left with their

Clubwomen banded together to force creation of a national forest. *(St. Paul Pioneer Press, December 12, 1900)*

Pike Bay Road, Chippewa National Forest, 1938

allotments and the price of the land for the forest, as determined by the federal government.

What was achieved, however, was a precedent that would live on in the annals of Minnesota conservation. There were now those who were loudly, and publicly, pledged to halting the business of mindlessly chewing up and disposing of the natural resources of Minnesota, as it had been practiced throughout the nineteenth century. Further, these were studious activists who were willing to put forward their own rational, conservationist plans for a wiser usage of those resources. And, finally, it was entirely possible, for a captain of nineteenth-century industry, to have one of these loud and forceful advocates seated across from you each night at the dinner table.

Writing of the Chippewa Forest years later, Gifford Pinchot would say, "Here was the first application of Forestry to Government-owned forest in America. . . . Without the farsighted and patriotic support of the Minnesota Federation of Women's Clubs, it would have been impossible."

Sex and the Psychology Professor

I N THE SPRING OF 1895, first-year professor Harlow Gale decided to give a lecture on sexual instincts to his psychology class at the University of Minnesota. Gale understood that he was stepping on delicate ground with this subject — sexual psychology had never been a part of university instruction before — so he took the time to inform President Cyrus Northrop of his intentions. Either Gale was not explicit about what he was going to do or the content of his upcoming lecture failed to register with the president. Northrop gave his consent with his "characteristic passive acquiescence," Gale later wrote. Meaning he didn't pay much attention — at first.

Gale had arrived on campus with a Continental education in psychology and enthusiastic ideas about how he might employ it while teaching at the University of Minnesota. His psych studies — and the fact that they were conducted in Leipzig, Germany — put Gale at the forefront of progressive education in 1894, the year he joined the Department of Philosophy, where the study of psychology was housed. Gale was poised from the start to butt heads with nineteenth-century notions about how the sons and daughters of Minnesota ought to be educated. And the champions of those ideas were unimpressed by Gale's progressive thinking and that German education.

Despite a certain naïveté about the workings of a state university, Harlow Gale was no kid when he arrived on campus. Born to a well-heeled Minneapolis family in 1862, Gale had gone off to Yale for his undergraduate degree, returned to Minneapolis for a couple years of graduate studies in economics, and then gone back to Yale to study philosophy. His three-and-a-half-year sojourn in Germany began in 1890, when he was twenty-eight years old, and included research in physiological psychology, nervous disorders, and experimental psychology. It was as an instructor in this last subject that he was hired at Minnesota. Gale replaced the university's only other faculty member in psychology and quickly set up a laboratory for himself and his students. He began instruction in physiological psychology, child psychology, the psychology of sense and feeling, and the study of the psychology of advertising—a course that was the first of its kind in the nation.

Gale was devoted to scientific reasoning and to expanding the minds of his students through experimentation, demonstration, and Socratic methods that encouraged interchange between instructors and students. The University of Minnesota of that day was inching slowly toward the type of classroom that Gale created, but it still was heavily influenced by a nineteenth-century style of instruction that emphasized classical subjects (Latin, Greek, mathematics, and philosophy), rote learning, and a reliance on metaphysics rather than science to address the bewildering questions that inevitably arose in scholarly pursuits. Some answers were to be left in God's hands, a notion that students were expected to understand.

Matters like history, economics, literature, and psychology were new to the curriculum. So, too, was the sense that students might have minds of their own. Religiosity infused the university. This galled Harlow Gale as much for the dose of hypocrisy with which it was administered as for its presence at a public institution of higher learning. Faculty meetings opened with a prayer at which "only half a dozen of the veteran professors joined in . . . with any sincerity," Gale wrote in a lengthy defense of his teaching

Forward-thinking professor Harlow Gale, reading in his office after joining the university faculty, 1896

methods, which he later published as *Ideals and Practices in a University: A Pedagogical Experiment.*

Leading the faculty in these sessions and probably oblivious to the lack of devotion around him was university president Cyrus Northrop. Hired as the second president in the wake of William Folwell's tumultuous administration, Northrop arrived from a professorship at Yale. His assignment was to build the university and make peace between it and the various powers in the state that held influence over its course, including the Board of Regents, the state government, and the population in general. Northrop was a consummate political animal and proved successful in this role. "He endeared himself to the people, won support from every group, and as the years went by became the most beloved of all Minnesotans," wrote historian Theodore Blegen of Northrop.

Despite these gifts, Northrop had a few blind spots when it came to administering the university. He was far less inclined to be interested in the pedagogical theories of a young professor like Harlow Gale than he was in making sure the parents of some freshman from the piney woods of northern Minnesota felt their child would be safe and sound at the university.

The Board of Regents meeting with President Cyrus Northrop (in front of radiator), 1889 *(photo by Edward A. Bromley)*

Gale had known Cyrus Northrop for years prior to being hired. Northrop had attended the same Minneapolis Congregational church as Gale's mother and had actually taught Gale when he was a young student at Yale. To Gale, this last link was not a point in the president's favor. In his estimation, Northrop's teaching had epitomized a style designed to hammer home dull lessons "in the quickest and easiest way" possible, as Gale wrote in *Ideals and Practices*. Given Northrop's political sensitivities and Gale's stubborn idealism, it was probably inevitable that the two would clash. It happened first over the sex lecture.

Beginning with an explanation of the anatomy "of the powerful sexual centers," Gale's talk outlined "the sensations, feelings, and emotions" that arose from these centers and manifested themselves in "the vague longings and unrest" that come to humans with puberty. In other words, with a heavy emphasis on nerves and psychological anatomy, Gale was giving "The Talk" to his college underclassmen.

With a quick diversion into the "manifold psychological disturbances" caused by the repression of these sexual emotions (*Psychopathia Sexuelis*, by famed Austro-German psychiatrist Richard Krafft-Ebing, was one of the primary sources for the lecture), Gale finished his discussion by underscoring for his students that the most sublime expression of sexual emotions came through marriage. "The highest function of sex life was opposed to the gratification of temporary relations or promiscuous intercourse," he told them. Sexual ecstasy between man and wife, on the other hand, "brought [men and women] nearer together in giving an increased fullness, depth, and richness to their highest aesthetic and ethical sympathies."

The talk came and went—surprisingly smoothly, thought Gale—and an entire year passed. He decided that, since a number of his students appreciated his lecture, and no one had objected, he would do it again. He proceeded to give the same lecture in his second year of teaching. But this time a couple of new students—"YMCA zealots," in Gale's description—were left openmouthed by their psychology professor's frank discussion of human sexuality and rushed off to Northrop's office to tattle.

Suddenly, the president was fully cognizant of the implications of his psychology professor's lecture, and, again according to Gale's account, he was livid. "Armed with a written report of these alarmists," Gale wrote, "the president suddenly appeared in my study, out of breath and in tremendous excitement, to demand what I meant by all this scandal. He shouted that I had done more harm to the university than I could ever live to undo, that the rumors of this talk would spread like wildfire throughout the state, that he would never hear the end of it, and that the people of the state didn't send their boys and girls to the university to hear such irreligious corruption."

Physiology professor
lecturing an art class
about the human
body, 1890s

Gale tried to explain his thinking on these matters, but Northrop was so upset that "no calm discussion with the president was possible," Gale recorded. Northrop stormed back out of the office, leaving his psychology professor to contemplate his fate.

For the next few weeks, rumors of the notorious "sex talk" floated around the campus, but Gale heard nothing from the president. In his own defense, Gale sought out an unidentified regent and described the lecture. He was heartened to hear the man agree with "the facts and views" as presented by Gale but then was chagrined when he was also told that "a university is not the place to teach many kinds of truths." Among them, obviously, were those pertaining to sexual instincts.

A couple of months after Northrop had burst into his office, the president informed Gale that his contract was not being renewed. Gale asked for and received an opportunity to plead his case before a special faculty meeting, where he learned that, aside from his frank discussion of sex, Gale was being assailed also for his manner of instruction. It was too "materialistic," according to his critics. It lacked metaphysical overtones. It lacked a sense of the soul.

Gale offered an impassioned defense of his teaching methods and boldly stated that it was through science and reasoning that educational advances had been made in the past half century. He also promised not to give "The Talk" again to his students, and it was probably this fact, more than his passion, that got Gale his job back.

With this reprieve, Gale went about building a noteworthy, but brief, scholarly career at the university. Gale's study of advertising and its effects, which he published in an article titled "The Psychology of Advertising," in 1900, was the first time a psychology laboratory was used to examine the influences of advertising on consumers in a scientific fashion.

In addition, Gale was a devotee and scholar of classical music and wrote music criticism, beginning in 1903, for a local publication, the *Minneapolis Daily News*. And he and the extended Gale family helped build an aesthetic appreciation for both symphonic and chamber music in the city of Minneapolis.

All well and good, but Harlow Gale's difficulties weren't behind him. With his "materialism" and his demonstrated inclination to discuss sex in the classroom, Gale had left Cyrus Northrop's "circle of trust" and trouble quickly resurfaced. Two years after the first dismissal, Gale was let go again,

President
Cyrus Northrop
greeting graduating
coeds, 1906

this time because of intradepartmental strife. The chair of the Philosophy Department was an ally of President Northrop's, and Gale's hope was that by branching off into its own separate department, psychology could pursue its scientific course and leave the metaphysics to philosophy. This very thing was being done at universities across the nation. Gale, however, made the strategic mistake of going behind Northrop's back to petition the Board of Regents directly.

Gale described Northrop, in a face-to-face confrontation with him, as breathing fire: "You thought you'd got this scheme fixed up with the regents and could work it thru independent of me, did you?" Gale quoted Northrop. "I'll let you know that I'm running this university." Nor had Northrop forgotten the first contretemps between them: "You know you've been a stench in my nostrils all these five years?" Northrop said to Gale, in Gale's account. "The bad smell of that sex talk you gave years ago is still abroad throughout the state."

Sex talk aside, what really infuriated Northrop was Gale's lack of religious conviction: "You hide yourself in your annex up there [Gale's laboratory]; have no connection with the rest of the university; investigate petty things about color, proportion, rhythm; teach that pernicious materialism

Students relaxing together on the steps of a campus building, 1910s of Physiological Psychology; and try to undo with your irreligion all the Christian Idealism taught by your superior."

The president of the University of Minnesota then leaned toward Gale and shouted, "Do you believe in God?" As the professor stammered out a long-winded answer that included phrases like "primitive literal anthropomorphism" and "figurative conception," Northrop cut him off: "I can't stand a man who can't answer Yes or No. You're a disgrace to this institution!"

More astounding than Northrop's tirade was the fact that, in its wake, he rehired the professor once again. Maybe it was because of Northrop's "natural human sympathy and kindliness," which, Gale allowed, "were generously large where they were not artificially checked by his narrow education." Or maybe Northrop just needed to vent. In any case, Gale was soon back on the job. But neither of these men was inclined to change, which meant that Harlow Gale would continue to teach in his "materialistic" fashion and Cyrus Northrop would continue to find that instruction irreligious and profane. There were no more scenes between them that Gale bothered to record, but he remained isolated from the president and his colleagues in the Department of Philosophy.

When Gale finally left the university, it was more with a whimper than with a bang. In 1903, budget cuts imposed by the state meant that faculty would have to be let go. It was not surprising that a controversial sort like Harlow Gale would quickly be given the ax.

Gale worked for a time in insurance after leaving the University of Minnesota, but he was even less suited for the world of business than for the world of academe. In time, he found a post with the city of Minneapolis, inspecting brickwork in area sewage systems.

The lack of glamour in his new career aside, Gale remained an interesting fixture around the community. He continued to live in the shadow of the university, where he kept a small lab, conducted experiments, and entertained students interested in psychology and progressive education. He had many friends outside the university, including the famed muckraking journalist Lincoln Steffens, who was a lifelong correspondent. Gale wrote a few scholarly articles, some fiction, and music critiques; served as secretary for the Minnesota Academy of Science; and dabbled in Socialist Party politics in Minnesota. He also wrote and published his parting shot at the university, *Ideals and Practices*, in 1904.

No doubt he occasionally bumped into Cyrus Northrop, too, who continued to head the university until 1911, when he finally retired as the longest-tenured president in university history. It would take another six years after Northrop left office before the University of Minnesota began plans to create a psychology department, which would finally be established in 1919.

The Fight for Academic Freedom

THE FAMED SCOPES MONKEY TRIAL in 1925 dramatically captured the simmering debate between those who believed in the right to teach the science of evolution and those who believed that the teaching of evolution was poisoning the minds of young people against their Christian heritage. The principals in that epic struggle were Clarence Darrow, who defended high school teacher John Scopes against charges that he had broken Tennessee law by teaching evolution in his classroom, and the aging William Jennings Bryan, three-time Democratic nominee for president of the United States and a former secretary of state during the Wilson administration. Bryan was also the leading figure in the Protestant fundamentalist movement, which emphasized a literal interpretation of the Bible.

The outcome of that classic trial is well known: Darrow lost his case but won the argument, while Bryan won the suit and lost his life (dying in his sleep five days after the trial's conclusion). What is less well known is what happened to the evolution debate afterward. In fact, it came north and landed in the state of Minnesota, right on the doorstep of the University of Minnesota, where the ensuing brawl between fundamentalists and the university community would unite students, faculty, administration, and the maturing alumni association behind the cherished right to academic freedom.

William B. Riley, pastor of the First Baptist Church in Minneapolis, was the most famous minister of his day in Minnesota and one of the leading figures in the fundamentalist movement. Riley was a tall, handsome man, charismatic and a fierce debater. He had arrived in Minneapolis just before the turn of the century and had grown First Baptist from a congregation of about six hundred to three thousand by the 1930s. He founded Northwestern College and Northwestern Seminary in the Twin Cities and also headed the

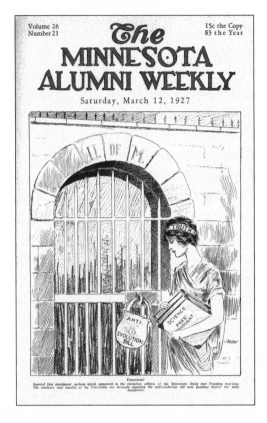

World's Christian Fundamentals Association (WCFA), a national coalition of churches formed to counter what it saw as a swing toward modernist thinking in American society, including the teaching of evolution in schools. Riley edited the WCFA organizational magazine from his offices at Northwestern College, and it was the WCFA that lined up William Jennings Bryan as the prosecuting attorney in the Scopes trial.

In the 1920s, a handful of southern states, including Tennessee, banned the teaching of evolution, but no northern states had similar proscriptions. In the wake of the Scopes trial, fundamentalists resolved to spread the ban above the Mason-Dixon Line, and William B. Riley's presence in Minnesota made the state a likely target. The anti-evolutionists, or simply the "antis," as they became known around the university, had already fired warning shots on campus in the early 1920s.

Inspired by a lecture visit to Minnesota by Bryan in 1922, Riley and other like-minded pastors formed the Minnesota Anti-Evolution League. The next spring, a number of Presbyterian ministers, backed by Riley's group, sent a letter to President Coffman demanding that the university investigate and remove from its syllabi any books containing references to the teaching of evolution. They cited two specific examples, including a history by H. G. Wells.

Coffman very politely declined the ministers' request in a personal letter, saying that no students had yet complained about these texts and that it was doubtful that much of this reading even sank in with modern students. "Indeed, I can say to you, that it is surprising to one not familiar with students, how they can skip things in a book; sometimes they can miss most that is between the covers," the president wrote. Later in the letter, however, Coffman did get around to what would soon be the crux of the matter with a lengthy discourse on university efforts "to achieve a free and liberal intellectual spirit in its method of instruction." Still, the overall sense in Coffman's response was his hope that the fundamentalists would just go away.

Members of Minneapolis's First Baptist Church, including the state's leading anti-evolution critic of the university, William B. Riley (in striped tie, first row, center) *(photo by Charles Hibbard)*

They didn't. "The Antis Are At It Again," screamed a March 1926 headline from the *Minnesota Alumni Weekly*, eight months after the 1925 Scopes trial. The occasion was the cancellation of a lecture by Riley on campus. Riley had originally been granted permission to speak, but he had slightly misled Dean of Administration F. J. Kelly about the nature of his topic. When Kelly discovered that Riley was advertising his talk with the inflammatory title "Should the Teaching of Evolution Be Longer Tolerated at This State University?" rather than the simple "The Fundamentalist Side of the Question of Evolution," the dean withdrew the invitation.

Riley was not a man to take rejection lightly. For the next several months, he and the Anti-Evolution League took to the state's highways and byways, damning the university and drumming up support for legislation that would prohibit the teaching of evolution in all of Minnesota's public schools. The university was feeling some heat. In an attempt to smooth ruffled feathers, Kelly and Coffman agreed to let Riley speak on campus, when he was asked again the following November. They even allowed not only one, but four lectures.

But these engagements served only to spur Riley's resolve. In the first of these talks, held before a raucous crowd of three thousand at the University Armory, one waggish student in the balcony lowered a stuffed monkey on a string in front of Riley's face as he began his speech. The laughs that ensued typified the student body response to the antis.

But a few months later, in March 1927, legislation that would make it "unlawful for any teacher or instructor in any public school, college, State Teachers' college or University of Minnesota supported in whole or in part by the public education funds of the State of Minnesota to teach that mankind descended or ascended from a lower order of animals" was making its way through the state Capitol. Word was that many rural legislators were inclined to agree that the theory of evolution should not be taught in Minnesota's schools. This meant that the University of Minnesota—as well as all higher-education institutions across the state, and perhaps the nation—were suddenly faced with the prospect of state legislators, and their pastors, dictating school lesson plans. Suddenly the monkey wasn't nearly so cute.

Since its inception in 1904, the General Alumni Association of the University of Minnesota had been unafraid of jumping into the political arena. In fact, it had been founded in a political fight between the state and the university over who controlled the school's budgets. The state had instituted a Board of Controls to oversee the day-to-day finances at the university, which meant that every nickel spent by department heads was scrutinized by an accountant at the state Capitol. This was just plain wrong, cried the newly

formed alumni association, taking its grievances directly to St. Paul. A sympathetic ear and redress were found in Governor John Johnson's office, and
by 1905 the Board of Controls no longer controlled university funds and the
alumni association was puffing its chest.

By the late 1920s, the alumni association was less inclined to leap whole-
heartedly into a donnybrook. But it made an exception in the case of Riley's
legislation. "Evolution Fight Calls Alumni," trumpeted a March 1927 *Alumni
Weekly* headline. "A serious blow has been struck at educational freedom!
Minnesota alumni therefore are called to arms to present forcefully their
views to the state legislature. Rarely in the history of Minnesota education
has so serious a crisis existed which called for immediate and concerted
action on the part of the intelligent—and we mean the laymen as well as
the so-called intelligentsia—people of this state."

Defense lawyer
Clarence Darrow
(left) and an
unidentified man,
at the Minneapolis
Auditorium in 1925,
the year of the Scopes
Monkey Trial

The question was not whether one side was right or wrong in the evolution debate. The issue was tolerance: whether, as stated in the *Alumni Weekly,* "certain groups [could] force their beliefs upon the multitude through the aid of the strong arm of the law."

Students took up the same cry, as did the faculty and the administration. On March 8, 1927, the day the state Senate Education Committee was set to begin proceedings for a public hearing on the bill, the All-University Student Council declared "a campus emergency." Classes were dismissed at noon and a mass meeting was held at the Armory, during which squads of students circulated petitions against the legislation. The meeting was said to have attracted 5,000 of the 9,600 students then enrolled at the university, and hundreds reportedly were turned away.

The next day at the Capitol, the scene was equally wild. Both Coffman and Riley were scheduled to testify on the merits of the bill. The great issue here was academic freedom, said Coffman, who began his testimony by recalling the territorial assembly that founded the University of Minnesota: "These men had a vision of a great commonwealth ministered to and served by the teachers of the University. Never once in those early years did they seek to limit the work or the activities of the University; never once did they seek to prescribe what it should teach and what it should not teach; never once did they seek to fasten upon it any special creed or doctrine."

Coffman kept swinging: "I am opposed to the bill for the reason that it is contrary to the genius of American life. . . . The spirit of America will wither and decay when the correctness of scientific theories is decided by legislation or by the counting of heads." And in closing: "Let the doubtful honor of striking a blow at free schools and the principles upon which our government rests pass to such communities and states as do not know to cherish and defend them."

By all accounts, Riley was not nearly as eloquent in his testimony. He also committed the cardinal sin of not having his facts in order. At the end of his speech, Riley claimed that despite what Coffman, the administration, the faculty, and the alumni of the university might say about the bill, the majority of students favored the legislation.

He got that wrong. The next speaker was Howard Haycraft, editor of the *Minnesota Daily*. Haycraft had with him "a long roll of paper containing 6,500 signatures opposed to the legislation," which had been collected at the student rally the day before. Haycraft presented the roll to the committee and also reported that, at the rally, a vote was taken on a resolution condemning the proposed anti-evolution bill. It was passed unanimously.

Rarely before, and rarely since, had the university community acted in such a concerted fashion. The strength of its collective voice impressed the statehouse crowd in St. Paul, and the next morning the Senate voted fifty-five to seven to kill the legislation. The Anti-Evolution Bill was dead in Minnesota and would never rise again. Academic freedom, it seemed, was no monkey on a string.

Still, William B. Riley was hardly cowed. He continued to be one of the leading voices in the national fundamentalist movement, even as he tended to his congregation in Minneapolis and oversaw Northwestern College and Seminary.

A FOOTNOTE TO HIS STORY: As he was nearing death in 1947, Riley handpicked his successor at Northwestern, a promising young minister named Billy Graham, whom Riley had first met in 1944. According to his own account, Graham was somewhat reluctant to take the post but had a hard time turning down the forceful William B. Riley. Graham served as president of the Northwestern schools for the next three years before going on to wider fame.

No Other Moment Like This One

I N FEBRUARY 1950, Bill McMoore (B.A. '51) of the University of Minnesota boxing team received a front-page apology in the *Minneapolis Tribune* from the school's president, James Morrill. The light heavyweight had been kept home from a team trip to Miami because coach Ray Chisholm said he wanted to rest McMoore for an upcoming Big Ten bout with Michigan State. In truth, the stay at home was prompted by Florida boxing rules that prohibited white fighters from facing black fighters in the ring. The boxing team wasn't interested in making an issue of the matter.

It won't happen again, Morrill told McMoore through the newspaper. "The right of a home team to prescribe conditions of athletic contests on its own campus has been generally recognized in intercollegiate competition," he wrote, "but the University of Minnesota cannot participate if those conditions are contrary to its own fixed policy." The Minnesota boxing team, which was in Miami at the time of the announcement, would be allowed to compete, said Morrill, but it would be a last time for Gopher athletics teams. "No further intercollegiate contest will be scheduled under circumstances that might bar eligible members of its teams from participation."

In the years following World War II, the segregation that had characterized prewar campus race relations was becoming an embarrassment to much of the university community. But black students remained isolated, and an uneasy future loomed. The student body as a whole had changed. The University of Minnesota was teeming with new students, many of them war veterans, many with families, and many in need of housing. But African American students were still few and far between, and most concerns expressed toward their well-being on campus came in the form of studies that documented what black people already knew: namely, that discrimination was firmly embedded in the life of the campus and the community around them.

Students on the university campus in front of the Physics Building and Northrop Auditorium, 1946

A 1948 survey from the Office of the Dean of Students, for instance, indicated that twenty-seven student organizations at the university—almost all of them fraternities and sororities—had restrictive clauses expressly prohibiting Negroes from joining them. Housing remained a problem as well. It wasn't until 1950, at the prodding of the NAACP, that the university quit asking its approved roster of landlords to list religious and racial preferences for renters.

Like so many other students of the era, McMoore had arrived at the University of Minnesota, in 1946, after a two-year stint in the U.S. Army. A graduate of Minneapolis South, he was the first member of his family to earn a high school diploma and would become the first to graduate from college. At the university, he majored in education and was the only black person in the department. "That wasn't anything new to me," McMoore says. "I was the only black player on the football team and the only black boxer too."

McMoore remembers that the football team played no southern schools during his stint at the U of M and that he roomed by himself on the road, until teammate Ted Christiansen volunteered to bunk with him. When he graduated in 1951, McMoore couldn't immediately find a job in the Minneapolis school district. (A 1947 "Survey on Human Relations" conducted for the city of Minneapolis showed that in all 121 Minneapolis public schools, exactly one African American was employed, as a clerk. There were no black teachers in the system.) McMoore spent two years working as the athletics director at a community house in St. Paul and then earned his master's degree from a school in Missouri.

McMoore returned to Minneapolis in 1958, when "the district was finally willing to hire me," he says. He spent a number of years teaching at Minneapolis South before becoming director of health, physical education, and athletics for all Minneapolis schools, a position from which he retired in 1989. He spent another half-dozen years in the 1990s working as manager of community relations for the Minnesota Timberwolves. Of his years at the university, McMoore says, "I learned never to quit. My experiences helped me to just keep going in life."

Clarence Taylor (B.A. '62) arrived at the U of M from St. Paul Central in 1958 and was soon recruited into one of the university's first attempts at educating itself and the community about matters of diversity: a branch of a nationwide student organization called the Panel of Americans. Instituted at UCLA during World War II in response to the wave of anti-Japanese sentiment that came with the onset of war, the Panel of Americans sent groups of students of diverse religious, racial, and ethnic backgrounds into the community to discuss their experiences and to educate Minnesotans about their differences. The University of Minnesota's branch of the organization

Boxer Bill McMoore advanced
to the NCAA semifinals
with the best team record, 6–1.
(1951 Gopher *annual)*

was first suggested in 1954 but didn't get off the ground until 1958. Taylor was one of the first African American students enlisted.

"Basically we went all over the Twin Cities and out-state too," says Taylor, a retired sales associate from Twin Cities–based Best Buy. "There'd be five students on each panel, and we'd speak about our experiences and then answer questions: 'Do you feel like outcasts? What do you think about Martin Luther King? Would you ever date a white woman?'"

The panel would also typically include a Jew, a Catholic, and a member of a large Protestant faith, along with a person from less well-represented racial, ethnic, or religious groups on campus, including Native Americans, Asian Americans, Mormons, and Unitarians. The Panel of Americans would exist at the university into the late 1960s, and through the years it visited hundreds of high school assemblies, fraternities, sororities, women's clubs, and Sunday school classes.

The civil rights movement itself was just beginning to be a presence at the University of Minnesota during Taylor's years, and he recalls numerous campus conversations about sit-ins and being a part of an early civil rights organization called Freedom Minnesota. But African Americans at the university were still isolated, and—with the exception of a group of star football players—they kept a low profile. Like Taylor, they tended to live off campus.

The football players included Sandy Stephens, Judge Dickson, Bob Bell, Bill Munsey, and Bob McNeill. They were a part of the program's first major effort at recruiting black athletes and would help carry the Gophers to the 1960 Big Ten championship and back-to-back trips to the Rose Bowl, including a 1962 victory. Stephens was the nation's first black all-American quarterback; Bell would also receive all-American honors and go on to a great pro career as an all-star tackle.

The Gopher basketball team was not as quick as Murray Warmath's football program to recruit African American players. It wasn't until 1963 that the university awarded scholarships to its first three black players, the extremely talented trio of Lou Hudson, Archie Clark, and Don Yates. That was the same year Clarence Taylor's brother, David, arrived on campus. David Taylor (B.A. '67, Ph.D. '77) was one of a very few African American students in the College of Liberal Arts and was a little overwhelmed by the sheer size of the university and the lack of kindred souls on campus. "I would go for days without seeing another black student," says Taylor. "We were basically dumped into the masses at the U and told to make do. There were no scholarship programs for African American students, no cultural programs, no attempt to recruit students of color."

"I would estimate that there were about 50 or 60 African Americans on the campus at that time," says John Wright (B.S. '68, M.A. '71, Ph.D. '77), who also arrived at the university in 1963. "There were more international students from some individual countries than there were African Americans."

Gloria Williams came to the University of Minnesota the same year as Clarence Taylor, in 1958. She held a master's degree from New York University and had taught in elementary schools in Boston before entering the doctorate program in the School of Home Economics at the university. She was hired as a teaching assistant and assigned to the Department of Textiles and Clothing. "I always felt a little isolated on the St. Paul campus," she says. "I still do." Williams has taught for over forty years in what has now become the College of Human Ecology. She received her doctorate in 1975 and sent a

Quarterback Sandy Stephens became the nation's first black all-American quarterback.

Professor Gloria Williams helped mediate the African American student takeover of Morrill Hall in 1969. *(photo by Mark Luinenburg)*

daughter, Kate, to the university. She recalls that during the 1960s there were just a few African American faculty and staff members at the university—the School of Social Work hired the first black woman faculty member, Ruby Pernell, in 1954—but there was no precise count.

Likewise, determining the precise number of black students remained difficult. Matt Stark (M.A. '59) began his career at the university in 1952, doing graduate work in educational counseling under the dean of students, E. G. Williamson. Stark became coordinator of counseling for U of M residence halls in 1954 and then was hired in 1963 to head a new human relations program established within the Office of the Dean of Students. In this last position, Stark would serve as adviser to a number of African American groups through the years, and he recalls making perhaps the university's first effort at creating a record of black students on campus. His admittedly unscientific methods included buttonholing African Americans he didn't know and simply asking them who they were.

Through his office, Stark guided a number of student civil rights and educational programs during the tumultuous years to come, including the Panel of Americans; Project Awareness, a program designed to aid "the educational enrichment and vocational motivation" of Native American youth; and the SCOPE (Summer Community Organization and Political Education) project, which was the famous—and perilous—voter registration drive of Martin Luther King's Southern Christian Leadership Conference. With the guidance of the Human Relations Office, student groups brought to Minneapolis a string of national civil rights and Black Power figures, including King, Hosea Williams, and Stokely Carmichael, for talks and convocations.

Nationally, there was an increasing sense of anger and frustration within black communities regarding continued racial injustices and the slow pace of change. The powerful legacy of Malcolm X, the emerging Black Panther movement, and a growing acknowledgment—culminating in the urban riots of the mid-1960s—that racism was not limited to southern states led to an escalating tension that was felt deeply on the campus of the University of Minnesota. "As the scene shifted from south to north, student organizations reflected the change," says Wright. "We started to look closely at the institutions around us."

In November 1966, an organization called Students for Racial Progress (STRAP) was founded at the university. According to one of its early leaders, Scotty Stone, in a *Minnesota Daily* article from January 24, 1967, the purpose of the group was to "stress self-directed progress" and put "more emphasis on the Negro and his relationship to his internal setting."

In spring 1967, STRAP sponsored Carmichael's visit to campus. That fall, Stone and other STRAP leaders led a demonstration that disrupted the opening convocation of the school year. The protest began with a silent sit-in in the front aisle of Northrop Auditorium during the program and ended with speeches and a tussle on the plaza outside Northrop. The ostensible reason for the protest was that an invitation to the convocation had not been extended to Ida Elam, the president of STRAP. But the deeper issues centered on the frustrations felt by black students with their isolation on campus and the lack of regard and respect shown them by the university. More disruptions were on the way.

In the winter of 1967–68, STRAP changed its name to Afro-American Action Committee (AAAC). The organization continued to grow, and new student leaders, like Rose Mary Freeman (B.A. '70), Horace Huntley (B.A. '70), and John Wright, emerged. By the time of Martin Luther King's assassination in April 1968, AAAC was a force to be reckoned with. "There had been a great deal of grousing on campus for a long time," recalls David Taylor, "but until AAAC came along, it tended to be non-directional."

"It's also important to note the town-gown connection," Wright says of the increased politicization of the black student body. "We found encouragement and support through African American community organizations like the Urban League, in the community centers like Phyllis Wheatley and Hallie Q. Brown, and through the Way, led by Mahmoud El-Kati."

In the wake of King's murder and a mass demonstration that followed, AAAC created a list of seven demands that it presented to university president Malcolm Moos. Drafted by Wright, these included an insistence that two hundred full scholarships be granted African American high school students from Minnesota in Martin Luther King's name; that guidance, counseling, and recruitment agencies be established and geared toward black students; and that an educational curriculum be established at the university "that would reflect the contributions of black people to the culture of America." In response, Moos and the administration began raising funds for a scholarship program to begin in the fall, established a Task Force on Human Rights to examine racial issues on campus, and formed a faculty committee to begin work on a "minority studies program."

Through the course of the summer, Wright and others helped recruit black students for the newly created scholarship program. But there was confusion about whether the scholarships were solely for African American students or for low-income students in general and if they were to be fully funded grants or scholarships supplemented by loans. In addition, the pace

Students Rose Mary Freeman, Horace Huntley, and Tucker Warren Jr., after the Morrill Hall takeover that forced formation of the Afro-American and African Studies Department

established by the faculty committee for creating an Afro-American studies curriculum seemed glacially slow to black students.

By January 1969, AAAC had decided some action was needed to prod the administration. On Monday, January 13, seven representatives of AAAC visited Moos's office in Morrill Hall and presented a list of three demands to the president that they said needed to be met immediately. They asked that an Afro-American studies program be established by fall 1969, that the university contribute one-half of the cost of a proposed national conference of black students to be held in February, and that control of the Martin Luther King scholarship program be placed in the hands of an agency of the black community. Moos was given until one o'clock the following afternoon to meet the demands.

The next day, seventy AAAC members gathered in Moos's office. Moos met with the students briefly but had no answers that could satisfy their demands. Led by Freeman and Huntley, the students left the president's office, but instead of exiting the building, they simply went down a floor and took over the admissions office. In the evening, they were joined by about eighty white students, mostly members of Students for a Democratic Society (SDS). Morrill Hall was occupied, and it would remain so for the next twenty-four hours.

In all the years that African American students had been at the University of Minnesota, there was no other moment like this one. For the first time in the school's history, its attention—the attention of the administration, faculty, alumni, the rest of its student body, and the state's citizens—was focused intensely on the university's African American students.

Gloria Williams had never been contacted by the president's office before. Now she was asked to help mediate the situation. "When I was called to Morrill Hall, I didn't even know the president knew I worked on campus," she says. Williams grabbed an old, fur-collared coat and went down to the administration building. "In case I had to spend the night," she recalls, "I thought the collar would make a good head rest." She entered the bursar's office, where the SDS members were centered, and then walked toward the admissions office, where a chair barred the door. She knocked, and a skeptical face greeted her. Then someone from inside called, "That's Kate's mother!" and Gloria Williams was let inside, where she saw her daughter among the protesters. "I stayed for a while and talked with the students," Williams says. "It seemed to me they knew exactly what they were doing, so I left."

Through a day of back-and-forth negotiations between black students, administration officials, and community intermediaries, a settlement was hashed out. Administrators agreed to accelerate the pace of the creation of an Afro-American studies department, agreed to an AAAC presence on the Martin Luther King scholarship committee, and agreed to fund the February student conference. The black students agreed to leave the building.

There were recriminations. Moos came under intense criticism in some quarters for his handling of the situation and for acceding to student demands. Some $11,000 damage was done to the offices of Morrill Hall, though it remains disputed just who did the destruction (black students or the SDS). A commission was formed by Moos to investigate the circumstances of the takeover. And in March, a Hennepin County grand jury indicted Freeman, Huntley, and Warren Tucker and charged them with riot, criminal damage to property, and unlawful assembly. In the ensuing two-week trial in October and November 1969, Warren Tucker was acquitted of all charges and Freeman and Huntley were acquitted of felony charges of riot and criminal damage and given a year's probation for the misdemeanor charge of unlawful assembly.

When the dust settled, a fresh landscape at the University of Minnesota was revealed. By June 1969, the university's Board of Regents had approved a new Department of Afro-American and African Studies, and by 1970 courses were being offered within it. El-Kati, Earl Craig, Josie Johnson, and Lillian Anthony were hired as faculty. They would soon be joined by Anita Brooks (M.A. '71, Ph.D. '77), Reginald Buckner (Ph.D. '74), and Geneva Southall in

Clarence Taylor (left) was a pioneer in the university's self-education about diversity in the early 1960s. His brother, David (right), one of the few African American students in the College of Liberal Arts in 1963, became dean of the General College. *(photo by Mark Luinenburg)*

an interdisciplinary program that covered subjects that ranged from jazz to African history to the sociology of the African American family.

Some of the first to benefit from the program were those who had struggled to create it. John Wright, the son and nephew of 1930s graduates of the university, switched from engineering to American studies, then earned an appointment as an associate professor in the new department. He would eventually become the chair. Horace Huntley became a history professor at the University of Alabama–Birmingham. David Taylor served as dean of the General College at the University of Minnesota from 1989 until 2005, when he became provost at Morehouse University in Atlanta.

The corps of African American faculty and graduate students in the program created on campus a community that had never existed before: a thriving intellectual assembly dedicated to the study and enhancement of the African American community. Since its inception, the Department of Afro-American and African Studies has stood central to the intellectual and cultural life of African American students—and enriched the larger community at the University of Minnesota.

To the World

Students studying and researching in the university library, 1900s

The Ph.D. and the
Northeastern Fisheries

CHARLES BURKE ELLIOTT was a struggling young Minneapolis lawyer, working as a part-time editor for West Publishing Company to supplement the income from a legal career that was going nowhere fast. In 1885, he decided to jump-start his future by becoming the University of Minnesota's first candidate for the degree of doctor of philosophy. That plan turned out to be the initial step toward brief and unexpected renown in the nation's Capitol.

There was a touch of audacity in the idea; Elliott didn't even have a bachelor of arts degree. But he had studied at Marietta College in Ohio and was a brilliant law student at the University of Iowa, where he took a degree in law (it was possible, at the time, to get this degree without having a B.A.). Further, he had published a number of well-received legal articles since his graduation, and he reasoned that these, along with his law degree, ought to substitute for the missing B.A. He approached Cyrus Northrop, recently appointed the second president of the University of Minnesota, with his idea, guessing that Northrop might be a man with a sympathetic ear. The new president had grand ideas about putting the still-small University of Minnesota on the nation's higher-education road map, and one way to do that was to boost a graduate program that had not yet produced a single Ph.D.

Not many colleges in the nation had. German universities, the model of educational enlightenment in the late nineteenth-century United States, had been minting doctors of philosophy for many years, and the usual pattern for aspiring American academics was to do their doctoral work in Deutschland. That had changed somewhat, beginning in 1861, when Yale awarded this nation's first three Ph.D.s. The trend continued in the 1870s, when Johns Hopkins University opened with the mission of promoting graduate

Charles B. Elliott earned the first doctor of philosophy awarded by the university, in 1888.

education in this country. Even so, in 1876 only twenty-five institutions in the United States awarded Ph.D.s, and these were handed out to a grand total of forty-four students.

Northrop was himself a Yale man and keen on raising the standing of the university around the country. Despite the B.A. problem, Elliott was an appealing candidate. His substitute credits were accepted in lieu of the degree. The young lawyer soon began his course of doctoral study.

Elliott's major field was to be history, with studies in Roman law, international law, and the constitutional history of England and the United States, with an emphasis on the diplomatic history of these two nations. Elliott would work under the direction of Harry Pratt Judson, professor of history; William Watts Folwell, professor of political science; and George Edwin MacLean, professor of English. It was a prestigious crew. Folwell, Northrop's predecessor as president, was already an institution on campus; Judson would one day serve as president of the University of Chicago; and MacLean would serve as president of the University of Iowa and the University of Nebraska. "From time to time I met these gentlemen at their homes, where my work was examined and reading directed," Elliott wrote in his unfinished autobiography almost fifty years later. "Each took great interest in his only candidate; each became a life-long friend."

By the second year of Elliott's studies, it was time to choose a subject for his dissertation. At Judson's suggestion, Elliott decided to write on the ongoing diplomatic controversy between the United States and Great Britain over the Newfoundland fisheries, specifically, the extent to which Commonwealth member Canada could claim proprietary fishing rights to the waters off Newfoundland.

The topic might seem distant to a midwestern lawyer, but it was pretty hot in 1886. From the birth of the republic, the United States and Great Britain had maintained diplomatic relationships that were sometimes bellicose, sometimes surly, and sometimes merely fussy. England tended to be arrogant in its foreign relations, and the United States tended to be thin-skinned. One of the bones of contention was the matter of fishing rights. And just as Elliott was deciding to write on the topic, President Grover Cleveland's administration made a treaty with Great Britain that "gave much dissatisfaction to certain elements in the United States," Elliott wrote.

Cleveland was a Democrat. The "dissatisfied elements" were mostly Republicans from the New England states. The conflict revolved around the question of what rights Americans had to fish in Canadian waters. Not surprisingly,

New England fishermen thought these were too few and Newfoundlanders said too many. In late 1886, Elliott went off to libraries in Washington, New York, and Boston to research the history of this question.

The contentions escalated as he studied. Canadian warships seized American fishing schooners and arrested crews for casting their nets in Dominion waters. To retaliate, the Republican-controlled U.S. Congress passed a bill in spring 1887 authorizing American ports to bar Canadian ships and goods. Hotheads began spouting off about the possibility of war, a prospect that a poetic editorialist for the *Detroit News* warned could change the map of North America:

> We do not want to fight,
> But, by jingo, if we do,
> We'll scoop in all the fishing grounds
> And the whole Dominion, too.

George E. MacLean, one of Elliott's advisers, who later served as president of both the University of Iowa and the University of Nebraska

Back in Minneapolis, Charles Burke Elliott was putting the period to his thesis with a cooler head. To his doctoral committee he presented a dissertation that turned out to be a careful and thorough examination of past fishing treaties signed between the United States and Great Britain. It tended to support the New England contention that terms of the major accord governing fishing rights in Canadian waters (the Washington Treaty of 1818) were generally unfavorable to the United States. Not only did Elliott's dissertation prove satisfactory to Judson, Folwell, and MacLean, but also "the University decided to publish and distribute it as sort of a public document," Elliott wrote.

It was now the fall of 1887, and in Washington, D.C., the Cleveland administration was trying to ease tensions over the fishing disputes by hosting a joint commission of British and American diplomats. Three representatives from each country began hammering out a proposed agreement that would appear in February 1888 as the Bayard-Chamberlain Pact.

But even as the negotiations were taking place, Republican senators were leery of a favorable outcome. Eighteen eighty-eight was a presidential election year, and no one on the Republican side of the aisle, including Minnesota senator Cushman Davis, wanted to hand Grover Cleveland the laurels for settling this ancient dispute. They didn't want to be seen as nakedly political about the matter either. What they needed was some sort of learned argument that could support their political goals, the kind of wonky ammunition that would one day become a familiar part of the modern political caucus's arsenal.

When Davis was sent a copy of Elliott's thesis, simply called "United States and the Northeastern Fisheries," he found just the right sword to help Republicans make a few thrusts at the Cleveland administration. Be cautious with the Brits, was Elliott's learned summation; they have taken advantage in the past. Davis quickly put a copy of the book in the hands of every one of his colleagues in the Senate, and it soon became the talk of the Capitol. Senators were making speeches in the chambers with Elliott's book propped open on their desks, freely quoting from this grad student from the University of Minnesota on the Senate floor.

Elliott received warm letters of praise from some of the leading political and intellectual lights of the day, including Massachusetts congressman Henry Cabot Lodge; famed historian and diplomat George Bancroft; and diplomats John Jay, a descendant and namesake of the original coauthor of the *Federalist Papers*, and James Russell Lowell, a former minister to England, who wrote, "I have read with great interest & instruction your History of the Fishery Question. It seems to me a thorough & fairminded statement of the whole business."

Senator Cushman K. Davis used Elliott's thesis on fishing treaties to urge caution when negotiating a new treaty with Great Britain.

Any doctoral student camped in some lonely library carrel can appreciate Elliott's sentiments on January 6, 1888, as he pondered the circumstances that had brought him and his work to the attention of so many notables. He kept a diary during these heady days. And on that Friday, he indulged himself by describing how, as a seventeen-year-old youth in Ohio, he began his first job as a teacher. Now, ten years later, he asked himself:

> Have they been successful years? I think I am safe in saying that they have not been altogether wasted. . . . Within a month I have received personal letters from some of the most distinguished men in the land, unsolicited, all speaking in flattering terms of my work. . . . Surely, without vanity, I may feel that there is some distance between the poor muddy youth of seventeen, standing on that hill side in Ohio ten years ago, and the young lawyer of 27 here in this great Western City. Senators of the United States did not then write to that youth, "You have done yourself and the State great credit."

In the modern age, Elliott would surely have been whisked away to Washington for a season in the sun: a round of interviews on the public affairs programs, testimony at Senate hearings, think tank offers to consider. But back in 1888, the clock was already ticking on his fifteen minutes of fame. Though Washington continued to debate the pros and cons of the Bayard-Chamberlain Pact, Elliott was left in Minneapolis with his wife, a year-old son, and his still-meager law practice.

And, oh yes, he still had the obligations of an upcoming oral examination to fulfill the requirements for his Ph.D.

During the height of his romance with the Senate, Elliott's enthusiasm for the doctoral work began to wane, and his diary notes growing frustration with the faculty: "During May I suppose I will have to pass an examination for my Degree of Ph.D. if the faculty ever get the matter arranged." And, "If they go to adding any further requirements I will withdraw as my time is too valuable to give much more of it to this kind of amusement."

But as the weeks and months passed and Elliott's celebrity faded, his obligations remained. His days consisted of mornings at the courthouse, afternoons reading, and evenings attending to family matters. He kept abreast of activities in Washington and continued to receive congratulatory letters for his book, but discussion of the Bayard-Chamberlain Pact ground to a halt in the Senate (the treaty would ultimately be voted down by Republicans in August 1888), and the fisheries matter was no longer Topic A in the Capitol.

By May, Elliott was back with his nose fully to the doctoral grindstone. And as the date for his oral exam neared, the man who just months before had been brimming with confidence and self-satisfaction, was suddenly weak-kneed: "Am very much disgusted with my Degree business," reads his May 21 diary entry. "Am unable to get time to study and will have to face a severe examination without the necessary preparation. I am a fair specimen of an ass, to attempt any thing of the kind while running a business at the same time."

Elliott's concerns turned out to be unfounded. On Saturday, June 2, 1888, he went to the home of Professor Judson, where he had supper with his examining committee and then proceeded to face their questions from eight o'clock in the evening until ten. He learned his fate just a half-hour later. Congratulations were in order for Elliott, who had just been awarded the first doctor of philosophy degree in the history of the University of Minnesota.

"It has been a long hard course of study," Elliott wrote in his diary that night before going to bed. "I am well pleased to be free from it."

Elliott remained in Minneapolis after his June commencement. There he began a long and distinguished legal career that included stints on the municipal bench for the city of Minneapolis and as a state supreme court justice, where he sat from 1906 to 1909. In that year, President William Howard Taft appointed him as a federal judge in the Philippines, and he spent the next several years in the Pacific, first on the bench and then as a cabinet officer. Elliott helped shape the judicial system in the newly democratic government of the Philippines.

In 1917, Elliott published a two-volume history of the relationship between the United States and the Philippines that was well received in scholarly and diplomatic circles. There is no record, however, of anyone passing out copies of it on the floor of the U.S. Senate.

Iron Mike,
dedicated to
university students
who served
in the Spanish-
American War

Iron Mike

On Memorial Day 1906, a large crowd gathered on the grounds opposite the University of Minnesota's Armory, on land later occupied by the Bell Museum. They had come for the unveiling of a sculpture dedicated to university students who had served in the Spanish-American War. On hand to offer speeches for the occasion were former governor Samuel Van Sant, current governor John Johnson, President Cyrus Northrop, and Professor Arthur E. Haynes, who was the driving force behind the creation of this monument, donating the first $10 toward its completion and serving as chairman of the committee that raised the remaining funds.

Also on hand was the sculptor herself, a thirty-five-year-old Bostonian, Theo Alice Ruggles-Kitson, who had already built a reputation as perhaps the nation's foremost creator of military monuments in a career that would stretch well into the twentieth century. As a woman, working in a field composed almost entirely of men, she had nonetheless thrived in her labors, winning numerous contracts for her heroic depictions of Revolutionary era, Civil War, and now Spanish-American War soldiers. As she was introduced to the crowd, there was heard "a lusty Ski-U-Mah" from the assembled students on the grounds, according to the next day's *Minneapolis Journal*, which reported that a similar cheer had been given to Dr. Haynes.

Shortly after ten o'clock, following a brief musical introduction by the university's cadet band and a song from a group called the Euterpean Club, "little Richard Pillsbury Gale," the grandson of yet another Minnesota governor (the late John Pillsbury), was given the honor of pulling the drapes from the statue. As buglers played reveille and the cadet artillery corps fired off a salute, the sculpture of an American soldier, circa 1898, was unveiled.

Set upon a six-foot-high granite pedestal, the soldier was himself a nine-foot-tall iron goliath. Dressed in khakis and wearing a slouch hat above an open-collared shirt with rolled-up sleeves, he was posed with his feet flat on the ground and his hips slightly cocked. His left boot inched forward of his right, as if he were taking a momentary break from a slog through the jungles of the Philippines. A rifle rested in muscular arms across his thighs, with a cartridge belt on his hips and a pack set against the small of his back, adding to the impression of a soldier pausing in the midst of some sort of reconnaissance.

Veterans of the Spanish-American War called themselves "hikers," in the same way that World War I vets were "doughboys" and World War II vets were "GI Joes." In fact, this statue, which would subsequently be recast more than fifty times and wind up in town squares and cemeteries across the nation, was given the name *The Hiker* in almost all of these locales, including at Arlington National Cemetery, where the monument was dedicated under that name in 1965.

On the University of Minnesota campus, where the very first casting of Theo Alice Ruggles-Kitson's statue was unveiled on that Memorial Day in 1906, the monument was called the Student Soldier Memorial, though, over the years, it has become popularly known among students as *Iron Mike*. Whatever its name, the sculpture memorializes the 218 University of Minnesota students who served in the war against Spain, including the nine who died in the conflict.

THE SPANISH-AMERICAN WAR came to the U of M campus in the same way that World Wars I and II would arrive: with a wave of patriotic fervor and a rush of young men to the enlistment rolls. Conflict between Spain and the United States had been simmering for many months prior to February 1898, when the U.S. battleship *Maine* was blown up in Havana harbor—by whom and how remains a matter of debate. What was important was that the United States, feeling its muscle and long tired of a Spanish presence in its spheres of influence, decided that the time was right to free Cuba of its oppressive colonial master. Spain was blamed for the destruction of the *Maine*, and by April the United States had declared war.

By April 23, the University of Minnesota student newspaper, the *Ariel*, was printing notice of a mass meeting at the Armory "for the purpose of considering plans for organizing a provisional battalion of volunteers from the University of Minnesota to be used in the service of the United States government against Spain." Very few Americans anticipated a lengthy conflict. Secretary of State John Hay would later write that what the nation had

Students served in the Thirteenth Minnesota, which debarked for the Philippines in June 1898.

needed at the time was "a splendid little war" to prove its rank in the imperial powers of the world. Spain, a weakening power with a weakening hold on distant colonies, was a perfect foil.

From the very beginning, one of the chief concerns of University of Minnesota volunteers was that they might miss out on the action. Most of the initial student recruits wound up in the Minnesota Thirteenth, a regiment that was organized and shipped to San Francisco before the month of May was through. Their final destination was to be Manila in the Philippines, another Spanish colony within the sphere of America's expanding influence and the second front in the war against Spain. But, of course, the Philippines were on the other side of the wide Pacific Ocean. Would the Minnesota Thirteenth even get a chance to fight after sailing halfway around the world?

"If blood tells and good looks go for anything, the men of Minnesota should be heard from in Manila," wrote a university student named Harry Currier from the Thirteenth's station in California. "That the Government expects well of them is proven by the fact that orders have been received to send them with the first Manila expedition," Currier wrote for the pages of the *Ariel*. "The Minnesota boys are magnificent. They are giants in stature, with fine clean-cut limbs and strong determined faces."

A few weeks later, as they shipped from San Francisco to Manila by way of Hawaii, those "magnificent Minnesota boys" were not looking quite so virile. Few of them had ever been to sea or knew its ignominies. "We had no idea a ship could roll so," wrote correspondent Currier. "The deck was often as steep as the roof of a house. . . . Long before we lost sight of land a good many of the boys had lost all interest in the scenery."

A good many boys lost more than that: "You would see one of them sitting very quietly by himself with a far-away homesick look in his eyes. Some kind friend coming along just then would inquire in a sympathetic tone: 'Sea-sick, Bill?' and would receive an indignant, 'No, feeling fine,' in reply. About five minutes later, Bill makes a wild rush for the rail, 'unable to contain himself any longer.'"

On July 5, the fleet containing the Minnesota Thirteenth reached Honolulu, where the Minnesota boys were entertained not only by the natives but by a Minnesota transplant named E. O. Hall and his lovely daughter Charlotte, who had attended the University of Minnesota in 1894, 1895, and 1896. She had pledged Kappa Alpha Theta, according to Currier. Hall was a wealthy hardware dealer with one of the most beautiful homes in the city. The most arresting moment in their stop, however, came at their arrival in Honolulu, when the Minnesota troops were greeted at the dock by crowds of native boys who dived for the pennies the soldiers flipped into the clear blue sea. To keep their hands free for their descents, the boys would put the

captured coins in their mouths, so that some "had their cheeks so full of pennies, that they looked like some new kind of pocket gopher."

The idyll of the Thirteenth in Hawaii was brief. By July 8, the regiment was once again at sea, heading across the Pacific for the Philippines, where it arrived on July 31 to curiously disappointing news. There in Manila Bay, the boys learned that Admiral Dewey had already destroyed the Spanish fleet two months earlier, in these same waters. In addition, the Thirteenth heard that Santiago, Cuba, had fallen while they were at sea. The war was essentially over before they had touched land.

As he and the regiment waited for their next orders, Currier reflected on the distance he and his fellow students had traveled: 2,100 miles from Minneapolis to San Francisco; 2,100 miles from San Francisco to Honolulu; and 4,918 miles from Honolulu to Manila. A total of 9,118 miles from home. They were not in Minnesota any longer: "The natives have bananas, oranges, pineapples, yams, eggs, live fowl and cocoanuts for sale, also several tropical fruits which I don't know the name of," wrote Currier to the *Ariel*. "They are very anxious to get Irish potatoes which they esteem a great luxury. Some of

Student soldiers, probably in Hawaii on their way to the Philippines, 1898 the boys got hold of a sack the other day, and did a thriving business, trading two potatoes for a dozen bananas."

The Spanish still had a tenuous hold on the city of Manila, but their principal concern seemed to be with Filipino insurgents, whom they had been fighting before the arrival of the Americans. Each night, Currier wrote, the Thirteenth could hear the Spanish lobbing shells at the guerrillas in the jungles surrounding the city.

Meanwhile, the Americans continued to wonder if there would be anyone to fight, after all these miles of travel. "Before this reaches you," Currier wrote to the editors of the *Ariel* on August 4, "the war may be over and we on our way home. If we remain here, however, I shall endeavor to tell in another letter something of the climate, people, and customs of the Philippines. I may note here that the weather so far, while it has been very rainy, has been quite cool and comfortable. The troops who came on the first expedition say that they have not suffered from the climate, except that it is very wet and muddy."

These were the last words of Currier's that the *Ariel* would publish. A week later, the newspaper sadly announced that it had received word of his death from typhoid fever in Manila. Harry Currier had been a junior from River Falls, Wisconsin, studying mining. "He was one of the popular men of the college," the paper added, "being of a genial, frank disposition and always ready for any fun or sport that might be going." Currier's death was one of four announced that week in the *Ariel*, including that of Sidney Pratt, who was the son of the mayor of Minneapolis. All had died of tropical disease, all had been members of the Thirteenth Minnesota, and all had made that long journey from the University of Minnesota Armory to the Philippines in the service of their country.

Meanwhile, Manila fell without much of a fight. American troops occupied Spanish barracks, and Spanish troops were imprisoned within the walls of the city. Members of the Thirteenth Minnesota were assigned police duty in the city, which would remain their principal role for the months to come. The Spanish were no longer a power on the islands, but the occupation of the Philippines would turn messy for the United States. In the years to come, American troops found themselves assuming one of the roles the Spanish had had in the islands—fighting the insurgency of Filipino guerrillas.

As fall turned into winter, and winter turned into the spring of 1899, Professor Arthur Haynes began his campaign on campus to honor the young students who had volunteered for service and who were even now serving 9,118 miles from home. He first suggested that a commemorative medal be sent to each University of Minnesota soldier, and then he proposed a monument.

ARIEL

Vol. XXII   UNIVERSITY OF MINNESOTA, MINNEAPOLIS, OCTOBER 1, 1898   No. 4

They Gave Their Lives

HARRY L. CURRIER

PAYSON COLWELL

SIDNEY PRATT

AUGUST FOSS

Among the nine university students who died in the war was Harry L. Currier, the *Ariel* correspondent who described the journey to the Philippines. *(Ariel, October 1, 1898)*

In the Philippines, the soldiers were grateful for the medals and thankful for the thoughts and prayers; but a year past the beginning of the war the Thirteenth Minnesota had had enough. In April 1899, the *Ariel* printed a letter from another former University of Minnesota student, Frank Force, who was serving in the Philippines: "From time to time we read in the papers that the troops are contented in Manila. This is not true, never has been true, and is written by some unscrupulous officer who has not the interests of his men at heart. The boys want to come home," he wrote. By the end of the summer, that was just what happened. Though an American force would remain in the Philippines for years to come, the Thirteenth was headed home, and Frank Force was soon back in Minneapolis, where he wound up as a newspaper reporter for the *Minneapolis Journal*.

In the meantime, Arthur Haynes continued his campaign to honor the university students who had served in the conflict. By 1904, he and his committee had raised sufficient funds to commission the work of Theo Alice Ruggles-Kittison, and the Student Soldier Memorial began to take shape.

Years after its unveiling, when the Bell Museum was built in the 1930s, *Iron Mike* was moved across the street to its current location in front of the Armory. There it continues to honor "the hikers" of the Spanish-American War and those, like Harry Currier, who never slogged through a Philippine jungle but nonetheless gave their all to their country.

Curiously enough, the statue has served another function through the years—a scientific and environmental purpose. Because *The Hiker* statues are so numerous and spread so widely across the country, they have been the subject of a National Park Service study that records the various levels of corrosion caused by acid rain in different regions of the nation. *Iron Mike* remains an ever-vigilant soldier, still slogging, in his own fashion, for the good of his country.

To Hudson Bay and Beyond

IN 1930, TWO RECENT GRADUATES from Minneapolis Central High School headed out on a journey straight from *Boys' Life*. Walter Port and his buddy Arnold Sevareid (B.A. '35), who would go on to fame using his middle name, Eric, when he worked for CBS News, baptized their canvas canoe the *Sans Souci*, in the waters of the Mississippi River near Fort Snelling on June 17. After paddling a few minutes south, they turned right at the Minnesota River and didn't look back.

To the source of the Minnesota River in Big Stone Lake, the young men paddled. From there, they headed on to Lake Traverse and the Bois de Sioux River. They navigated down the Red River, which they took all the way to giant Lake Winnipeg. From Lake Winnipeg, they steered out into the wilds of northern Manitoba, toward the ultimate goal of the trip: Hudson Bay. The route they chose to the bay, through rapids and rivers and lakes dotted with hundreds of uncharted islands, had only been traveled in its entirety by Native Americans.

When they got back to Minneapolis, Sevareid began his studies at the University of Minnesota and ultimately published *Canoeing with the Cree*, the story of his and Port's fourteen-week trip. Unless you count the message on the Runestone in Kensington, Minnesota, Sevareid's is the first fully recorded account of this particular journey in the history of adventure literature: more than 2,200 miles from the heart of Minnesota to Hudson Bay, by water and portage.

Reading the story today, it's hard to imagine a more knuckleheaded trip. The excursion from Minneapolis to Lake Winnipeg was primarily long and hard work, but the continued journey, on the great expanse of the lake and into the wilderness of Canada, was fraught with so much danger it's a minor miracle these two made it out of the woods alive. Just what made them think they could navigate uncharted waters in a territory they had seen only in their dreams is a mystery. Sevareid was so green he had never even been to the northern forest before he entered it.

To compound their own difficulties, the young men chose a route to Hudson Bay that not even the most experienced travelers in the region ever chose. At Norway House, at the northern tip of Lake Winnipeg, they took the counsel of a local trapper who told them that the Hayes River, the standard passage from the lake to the Bay, was low that year and that they would be doing less "wading and dragging" of their canoe if they opted to take a course that included God's Lake and God's River, a route that swung to the east of the Hayes.

Bad advice. Within days they were lost—not the last time that would happen in their journey into northeastern Manitoba. With the aid of a pair of Cree Indians, they found their way to God's Lake; but at the east end of this body of water, they found themselves off the map that they had borrowed from their trapper friend at Norway Bay. Just which outlet from God's Lake

Youthful paddlers Eric Sevareid and Walter Port, 1930

was God's River was anyone's guess. With God's good help they found it, but more terror and misery were on their way: rapids, god-awful portages, a constant rain. "Day and night, the drizzle did not cease for so much as an hour," Sevareid would write years later. "The woods oozed with water, every leaf held a pond, every dead twig and log was rotten with wetness."

In *Canoeing with the Cree*, Sevareid records that, time and again, strangers along the way told the young men that they would never make it—that they would freeze before they reached the bay or that they would get lost along the way. In Minnesota, these warnings sounded overly cautious, but by the time Sevareid and Port reached the northern sections of Lake Winnipeg, those voices sounded as sage as the Ancient Mariner's.

It's hard, too, to reconcile the image of the man Sevareid would become with the picture of the lad canoeing up the Minnesota River on his way to possible oblivion. To picture the older Eric Sevareid—dark eyes trapped under the hood of a melancholic brow, seated next to Walter Cronkite and delivering his evening sermon on the *CBS Evening News* in that distinct, clipped, and eloquent language of his—and imagine him as a young man in a high school English class daydreaming of canoeing with his buddy in the wilds of Canada seems a pretty far stretch. Yet they were one and the same person.

Sevareid and Port, beginning their canoe trip to Hudson Bay, 1930

Born in the small town of Velva, North Dakota, Arnold Eric Sevareid was the son of a banker who brought his family to Minneapolis when Eric was a teenager. In the city, Eric attended Central High and began his life-long career in journalism by working on the school paper and convincing George Adams, the editor of the *Minneapolis Star*, to underwrite his and Port's canoe trip to Hudson Bay. Adams agreed to pay the two young men $100 for periodic dispatches describing their journey, which were published in the *Star* through the course of that summer of 1930. These became the basis for *Canoeing with the Cree*.

Once back in Minneapolis, Sevareid took a job as a copy boy with another newspaper, the *Minneapolis Journal*, and soon entered the university as a night student. At the U of M, he wrote for the *Minnesota Daily* and became part of a group of liberal politicos who called themselves the Jacobins and successfully rebelled against, among other things, the requirement that all male students at the university have military training.

Sevareid studied political science with a minor in economics. He wrote a column for the *Daily* and took a number of journalism courses after his 1935 graduation. He hoped to spend that year as editor of the *Daily*, but another student won the position, a fact that left Sevareid bitterly disappointed, even after he had climbed to national prominence as a journalist. Already his brow was getting heavier. "When I read a novel of American campus life, or see a Hollywood version with its fair maidens in lovers' lane, dreamy-eyed youths in white flannels lolling under leafy boughs or lustily singing," Sevareid wrote in his 1946 autobiography, *Not So Wild a Dream*, "I am astonished and unbelieving, or I have a faint twinge of nostalgia for a beautiful something I never knew. I remember only struggle, not so much of 'working my way through' as the battle, in deadly earnest, with other students of different persuasion or of no persuasion, with the university authorities, with the American society of the time. I remember emotional exhaustion, not from singing about the 'dear old college' but from public debate."

It was perhaps only natural for someone with such a deep interest in public debate and journalism to wind up in the maelstrom that was Europe in the years before the war. After his graduation and a further stint with Minneapolis newspapers, Sevareid and his first wife, Lois, moved to Paris in the late 1930s. There he worked for a time as editor of the Paris edition of the *New York Herald* before being hired by CBS News to report on the escalating crisis in France as invasion from Hitler's Germany neared. Sevareid scurried around Europe, describing the looming war and impending fascist rule. When the French government capitulated, he joined Edward R. Murrow, his boss at CBS radio, in London, where he continued to report on the war until January 1941, when he was assigned the CBS news desk in Washington, D.C.

When the United States joined the Allied war effort, Sevareid badgered Murrow for an assignment in the field. He was sent, in 1943, to India to cover the U.S. Air Force's attempt to supply Chiang Kai-shek's Chinese army over the Burma "Hump" — the Himalayas. On one of these dangerous flights into China, the plane Sevareid was traveling in crashed behind Japanese lines in the Burmese jungle, and Sevareid and twenty survivors spent the next two weeks trekking 140 miles out of the broiling jungle. Of the arduous trip, Sevareid wrote in his journal, "It's the Manitoba canoe thing all over again."

Eric Sevareid, a popular news correspondent, about 1945

Out of China by the end of 1943, Sevareid returned to Europe and traveled with the U.S. Army during its invasion of Italy. He wound up the war with the army back in France and then Germany as the fighting came to an end in early May 1945. By June, he was heading home, where he took a leave of absence from CBS and immediately began working on *Not So Wild a Dream*.

The book was published to much acclaim in 1946. Meanwhile, Sevareid continued his work with CBS News, and in the 1950s he made the transition to television, with Murrow and others from that famed corps of CBS war journalists known as "Murrow's boys." He worked in Washington and London before joining Walter Cronkite in the 1960s as a commentator on the *CBS Evening News*. Sevareid became, after Cronkite, the most visible face of the most-watched news program on television.

To some, his essays, delivered to camera with no accompanying images (a lost form in the world of television news), could be frustratingly vague, offering a look at all sides of a question while refusing, ultimately, to answer it. To others, however, Eric Sevareid was an icon of sober judgment in wild times, a symbol of maturity and considered opinion in an age when these traits seemed sorely lacking.

Sevareid had come a long way from that summer spent canoeing toward Hudson Bay, a fact that he had recognized early on in his career. In *Not So Wild a Dream*, Sevareid was hard-pressed to find any great meaning in the trip he and his buddy Port had made. "We had paddled a canoe twenty-two hundred miles, had survived, and had proved nothing except that we could paddle a canoe twenty-two hundred miles, a capacity of extraordinarily small value for the future," he wrote. "My chief return on this investment, outside of a fleeting notoriety which got me a job on a newspaper — as office boy — was that for several months thereafter, until sedentary habits softened my flesh, my older brother could not lick me."

At the start of *Canoeing with the Cree*, it's pretty easy to agree with Sevareid's assessment. There seems to be no great purpose to this journey; we're simply traveling through a familiar land with a pair of pleasantly callow young men. Sevareid's descriptions of the landscape are vivid but offer few insights. His prose is clear and simple and very readable, but its most charming feature today is its description of a world gone by, where seventeen-year-old boys smoked pipes; wore knee-high, lace-up boots as they canoed; and were shy about their bare chests as they paddled into populated areas.

Even seen as a whole, the book lacks the traditional elements of a great adventure story. These young men could not have made it without the help of strangers, who guided them at various times along the way. But they are not "saved" on their journey. Nor are there any real heroics to be found. Nor does anyone seem to have a lot more wisdom coming out of the woods than going in. The highest moment of drama comes in the last few pages of the book, up in deepest, darkest Manitoba, when the two friends finally become fed up with each other and their own grand adventure. Lost once more on God's River, wet and chilled to the bone, Sevareid and Port wind up rolling around their camp in a wrestling match that somehow seems only natural, given their dire circumstances and the fact that they have only each other to blame for how they arrived there.

In the end, however, the two young men muddle through. And it's in the simple description of that muddling, faithfully reported by Sevareid, that *Canoeing with the Cree* transcends its *Boys' Life* roots and becomes not only a great story but a portrait of the brooding journalist to come. Sevareid simply can't make more of the tale than is there. So *Canoeing with the Cree* becomes a story of soggy blankets, aching muscles, and desperate, angry boys rolling around the smoldering campfire.

From these plain descriptions of desperate circumstances, however, comes a poignancy that kicks in subtly and flows all the way through the end of the book, when the boys, who have had to hitch a ride home from Canada, quietly return to their hometown.

On the eleventh of October Walter and I reached Minneapolis. We had left when the city was in the bloom of spring, buds were sprouting into new leaves and the grass was turning green, and the air was soft like rain water. As we walked toward home, our boots kicked up dead leaves that covered the sidewalks, the grass was turning into the drabness of fall, the smell of bonfires was in the sharp air, and smoke arose from the chimneys.

We went by the school, sitting on its terraces among yellow trees. As we drew nearer and nearer to home, high-school boys and girls passed us on their way to classes. We realized that we were looking at them through different eyes. We realized that our shoulders were not tired under the weight of our packs. It was as though we had suddenly become men and were boys no longer.

The most recent published account of Sevareid's 1930 journey by canoe to Hudson Bay

Port and Sevareid returned to Manitoba in 1980, three years after Sevareid's retirement from CBS News and fifty years after their initial canoe trip. Port had spent many of the intervening years living in Bemidji, where he worked as a photographer. Sevareid had been hired by *Audubon Magazine* to write a retrospective of their journey of 1930, and it was on the magazine's nickel that the pair traveled—by float plane, hopscotching from lake to lake—all the way to Hudson Bay.

Not just men now, but old men, the two of them got socked in by a fog for four days on the bay. They fished, talked, and got reacquainted after years of not being in touch. If there were any lingering problems between the two of them, stemming from that fight that marked the end of their first trip in this country, they were now gone. In *Audubon*, Sevareid wrote of dozing off for a moment and feeling Walter "arranging the fallen blanket over my exposed feet."

Even so, it was the last time the two voyagers would get together, and there is a haunting sense of irony about the whole return visit. So near death on their first journey to God's River, their return trip, even in the relative comfort of airplanes and lodges, suggested their shortening days. Port went home to Bemidji and died in 1994; Sevareid went back to a waning career in New York. Through the next decade, he would work on a pair of PBS documentaries, do commentary for National Public Radio's *Marketplace* and voice-over work, and make personal appearances.

On July 9, 1992, Eric Sevareid died in New York. Through one of the century's most distinguished careers in journalism, he had won three Peabody Awards and two Emmys, along with a host of other honors. In 1980, the University of Minnesota further honored him by christening the Eric Sevareid Library at the School of Journalism in his name.

That same year, he put a period to his first real writing assignment, that trip to Hudson Bay. In *Audubon*, he described flying over God's River fifty years after that first trip. "Rapid after rapid after rapid fled past us and I thought, 'My God, my God, how did we do it in the darkness and rain, in our innocence and ignorance?' The religious feeling does not often possess me, but now it did. Surely, Walter and I had rushed along those currents in company with some special blessing."

On the plane leaving the path of the river, he wrote, "God's River slipped behind us. I knew I would never see it again or need to."

Beneath Saudi Sands

I N 1932, a thirty-seven-year-old engineer employed by the Standard Oil Company of California (Socal) made a habit of climbing the highest point on the island of Bahrain, about twenty miles across the Persian Gulf from the Kingdom of Saudi Arabia. From that hilltop, he stared at the topography of the mainland, over the blue-green waters of the gulf. There, Fred Davies (B.S. '16), a University of Minnesota graduate in mining, saw a landscape similar to the one that he was standing on. In the distance, he could see a cluster of hills forming a dome above the countryside.

Davies had just drilled the first successful oil well in Bahrain through similar terrain. Now his training, experience, and instincts told him that there was more oil to be had across the water—much more—in those hills on the other side of the flat shoreline. In fact, he was confident enough in that assessment to advise his employers that they ought to be here, in the heart of Arabia, where no other oil company in the world had yet drilled.

It is no exaggeration to say that all of the momentous history that has subsequently linked the United States to the Middle East began with that appraisal. From it stemmed a series of events that brought U.S. oil companies to Saudi Arabia to begin extracting the single largest petroleum deposit in the world. From those wells have flowed billions of barrels of oil, trillions of dollars in commerce, and a steady stream of turmoil.

Fred Davies did not disappear from the story with those sightings. In fact, his work in Saudi Arabia, and at home in the United States for Socal (at his suggestion, the company name would be changed in the 1940s, to the Arabian-American Oil Company, Aramco), would make Davies one of the major figures in the early history of Saudi Arabian oil. From his days in the early 1930s as a "hunch and slog" prospector for oil in Bahrain to his retirement in 1959 as chairman of the board of Aramco, the largest producer

Fred Davies (second from left), at a camp east of Riyadh, Saudi Arabia, 1930s *(Special Collections, J. Willard Marriott Library, University of Utah)*

of crude oil in the world, Davies was an integral player in the world of oil discovery and development.

Born in Aberdeen, South Dakota, Fred Davies was raised primarily in north Minneapolis, one of five boys, whose father, Ralph, worked in the grain business in the city. The young Davies was tall, rangy, and handsome and earned the nickname "Slim" while studying engineering in the School of Mines at the University of Minnesota. Davies worked for the Anaconda Copper Company for a year after college, did a hitch in the military in World War I, working in a chemical warfare unit, and wound up employed by Standard Oil of California in 1922. There he looked for oil in the Rocky Mountains until he got the call to head to the Middle East. After overseeing the drilling of that first well in Bahrain and imagining the possibilities in Saudi Arabia, Davies made his first foray across the gulf waters to the mainland in spring 1932.

At the time, Saudi Arabia was just emerging as a modern nation. The Bedouin tribes, which had dominated the region for centuries, had been consolidated under the leadership of King Ibn Saud, and a monarchy, whose territory stretched from the Red Sea in the west to the Persian Gulf in the east, was formed. It was the heart of the ancient land known as Arabia and held the two cities most sacred to Muslims all over the world: Mecca, where the prophet Muhammad was born, and Medina, where the Prophet had died. Because of its importance as the religious center of Islam, Saudi Arabia was and remains a special land for all the world's Muslims.

In the early 1930s, King Saud was strapped for funds with which to govern his new nation and looked to the West for support through the sale of oil concessions. Historically, Britain had been the one Western power that had dominated the pursuit of oil in the Middle East, but its concessions and reserves had come from Iraq and Iran. It had never explored the interior of the Arabian Peninsula for oil. Though it seems hard to imagine today, there were questions whether oil even existed beneath these desert lands.

The British were dealing with a number of economic and diplomatic difficulties in the wake of World War I. Among them was their effort at maintaining a colonial empire under reduced circumstances. As a nation and economic power, Great Britain did not have the resources it once had had, and the upshot for King Saud was that Britain's interest in Arab oil exploration was surprisingly tepid.

The United States was a latecomer to the pursuit of Middle Eastern oil, but it jumped into the fray in the late 1920s. Socal had tried, with little success, to find oil in Mexico, Venezuela, Colombia, Ecuador, Argentina, the Philippines, and Alaska. Some within the company were less than enthusiastic about the prospects for oil in the Persian Gulf. These same skeptics viewed the exploration in even dimmer light as the Great Depression swept over the globe and a costly hunt for crude in Arabia seemed like an extravagance. Oil seekers within the company won out over its accountants, however, and Socal became the first American oil business to send explorers to the Middle East. Davies was the man picked to lead the crew, and Bahrain was the first site for drilling. After his successes there, Davies crossed into Saudi Arabia with the hope of talking to Ibn Saud about the possibility of exploring that dome of hills near the gulf coast for oil. But he failed to get an audience with the king and headed back to the United States empty-handed.

Ibn Saud's need for cash remained, British interest in the region's oil remained cool, and Davies, back in the States, continued to lobby for the exploration of oil in Saudi Arabia. Two new representatives of Socal were sent to the Middle East and won an audience with Saud in 1933. Through these emissaries, Socal was able to sign an agreement to begin the process of looking for oil in eastern Saudi Arabia. By 1934, Fred Davies was back in Bahrain. A year later, he was in Saudi Arabia, serving as camp boss in the first American effort at digging oil wells in those same hills that he had spied three years earlier, now called the Damman Dome.

As a nation, Saudi Arabia derived its income primarily from Muslim pilgrims making the trip to Mecca. Otherwise, Davies said in an Aramco statement, it was "a nomadic society [dependent] on the scant and uncertain provisions of the desert." The culture was tribal, patriarchal, Islamic, and ancient. According to Davies, it "could not have changed much since the days of the Prophet."

The agreement signed between Socal and the Saudis made patently clear that the Americans were in Arabia at the invitation of the Saudis and would adhere to the customs of the people and the land. That meant, among other restrictions, that alcohol was strictly forbidden and that consorting in any fashion with the women of Saudi Arabia was a crime punishable by death. In the eyes of the Saudis, the Americans were infidels, working in their lands at their own invitation and for Arab profit.

Into these circumstances came a group of roughnecks and wildcatters from Dust Bowl America accustomed to working in the oil fields of Texas, Oklahoma, and California. Cultural sensitivity was hardly their forte. Perhaps not surprisingly, all of the powers concerned felt it was best for contact between Arabs and Americans to be as limited as possible. Though Saudis provided much of the labor at the drilling sites, the camps themselves were isolated, and interaction between Americans and Saudis was otherwise strictly limited.

Davies's job was to make all of this work and to produce oil. He had the right, no-nonsense sensibility for the task. "Davies was not a terribly warm and chummy guy," wrote an Aramco colleague many years later, "but he was enormously respected by government officials and employees alike." Another co-worker said that he was "hard working, smart, imaginative, honest," and "concerned about people." Also, a little moody, said this friend, and quick-tempered.

No doubt working on the Damman Dome tested Davies's patience. Aside from the cultural difficulties, the desert climate was as extreme as any on Earth. Temperatures climbed quickly and easily into the 120s, and sandstorms were a frequent hazard. To top it all off, oil did not immediately pour from the sands of Saudi Arabia.

In 1935, Damman No. 1 was drilled in the dome and produced a modest amount of crude at 2,300 feet. A few months later, a second well, Damman No. 2, brought in oil at 2,100 feet. It began flowing at a rate of 3,800 barrels a day, which was a sufficiently exciting return for Standard Oil Company officials in San Francisco to send air-conditioning units to the camp in Saudi Arabia as a sign of commitment to the project. The company also quickly ordered drilling on Nos. 3, 4, 5, and 6.

But soon after Davies and the crew began working on Damman No. 7 in December of 1936, enthusiasm eroded. Oil from each of the first six wells had turned into trickles, and it would take until October for No. 7 to produce any oil at all—and that was at a depth of more than 3,600 feet. In early 1938, Davies and the chief geologist on the site were called back to San Francisco to explain to the honchos at Standard why it made sense to remain in the sands of Saudi Arabia.

Fred Davies (at left), president of Aramco (Arabian American Oil Company), with other officials *(Special Collections, J. Willard Marriott Library, University of Utah)*

The gusher came in while they were away. In March 1938, at a depth of more than 4,700 feet, Damman No. 7 started producing oil at a consistent rate of 3,000 barrels a day. After deeper digging in Nos. 2 and 4, oil came in at similar rates. All through the year, the crude was suddenly flowing thick and fast in the Arabian heat, and Standard Oil was finally convinced that it had struck pay dirt. Early in 1939, Ibn Saud and the nation of Saudi Arabia received its first royalty check at a rate of 21 cents per barrel, and soon after, the first shipment of Saudi oil was loaded into a tanker and headed for the United States.

Damman Dome was the first of more than fifty oil fields begun by Aramco in Saudi Arabia, where, in time, more than a quarter of the world's known oil reserves would be found. Damman Dome was not the largest field in the region, on land or sea, but it was where the saga of U.S. involvement in Middle East oil all began; and No. 7 would produce at a consistent rate of around 3,000 barrels of oil a day until 1982, a span of almost forty-five years.

Not long after that first shipment of oil sailed for the United States, Fred Davies followed it home. Back in California he was rewarded for his stellar work in Saudi Arabia by being named president of the Arabian arm of Socal. He held that post for the next seven years, overseeing the continued expansion of operations in Saudi Arabia.

Aramco was formed in the late 1940s out of a joining of Socal, Texaco, Exxon, and Mobil. At the time, Davies was asked to step aside from the presidency, which went to a Texaco man. Davies, "a good soldier," in the words of one co-worker, became vice president in charge of operations for Aramco and in 1949 moved back to Dhahran in Saudi Arabia with his wife, Amy, where the two would spend the rest of Davies's career. In 1952, the headquarters for Aramco were moved to Saudi Arabia, and Davies, already there and in charge of operations, was named chairman of the board and CEO. Along with the Texaco executive, who remained president of Aramco, Davies worked as a co–chief officer until his retirement in 1959.

The University of Minnesota honored Fred Davies in 1954 with an Outstanding Achievement Award for his professional accomplishments. Six years later, the university recognized Fred's brother Herman, also a University of Minnesota graduate (B.S. '21) and a longtime employee of Socal, with the same honor.

Davies spent the last years of his life in California, still working as a consultant, now for an oil development business called Kern County Land Company. In 1971, four years before his death, Aramco honored him by naming the first supertanker ever commissioned after him. The *F. A. Davies* delivered its first oil that same year. At ceremonies marking the occasion, he was honored as a man "whose vision, professional skills, and persistence were instrumental in the uncovering of vast petroleum reserves in the Gulf."

"What Is Our War Job?"

THE EVENTS OF DECEMBER 7, 1941, changed lives everywhere. When Japanese forces swept down upon Pearl Harbor, the nation's isolation ended. President Franklin Delano Roosevelt was soon speaking before Congress of "a day that will live in infamy," and the United States was suddenly at war. Just what being at war would mean to Americans, however, would take time to become apparent; and immediately after the declaration there were more questions than answers about what should be done and how lives were about to be changed by war.

Like many other organizations, the University of Minnesota's General Alumni Association was casting about for an appropriate role. Less than two months after Pearl Harbor, Ben Palmer ('11, '13), the president of the alumni association, began to define what purpose it would serve in the coming conflict. "What is our war job?" he asked rhetorically of alumni in an editorial in the *Minnesota Alumni Weekly* (January 24, 1942). "In this war, as never before, universities are recognized as mighty arsenals of ideas, trained personnel and research laboratories staffed by specialists in all fields." The University of Minnesota would be a national leader in this role, and, as such, Palmer wrote, "the university is now laboring under a dual responsibility. While making available its trained personnel and its facilities to the program of national war effort it must also maintain, as completely as possible, its normal educational function and its special services to the state."

Under the circumstances, the alumni association needed to continue doing the things it did well, said Palmer. It needed to "mobilize alumni and alumni opinion for effective action in the best interests of the University." Further, it should "make a contribution to the total war effort through a greater alertness to the problems and needs of the institution and assure the administration of our unified interest and support."

Navy recruits at a university football game, about 1942

In the next few editions of the *Alumni Weekly*, the alumni association began to show that support by highlighting what the university was doing to aid the war effort. A special edition of the magazine published in May 1942 described research efforts, pilot training and ROTC programs, the newly instituted Key Center of War Information and Training, and a War Conservation Program. The alumni magazine also offered its pages to President Walter C. Coffey, who began writing a regular column on war efforts and programs at the university. Alumni Day in June of that first year of war was given over to "acquainting [alumni] with the current problems of the institution" and reminding them that there were "opportunities for service to the University."

As things turned out, however, the alumni association would play a critical role in one particular area, where a pressing need soon emerged. "I am writing to inquire if the alumni office is taking any systematic steps to gather the names of former students and graduates who may have died in service," wrote Malcolm Willey, dean of the university, to E. B. Pierce, executive secretary of the alumni association, on August 31, 1942. Edmund Williamson, dean of students, was in the process of creating a record file of enrolled students who were casualties of the war, Willey informed Pierce. Similarly, "President Coffey would like to know the names of former students and alumni who have died in order that he may write their families."

It was a sensitive but crucial matter. Every day, more university students, faculty, and alumni were enlisting in the armed services. By the end of the 1942 school year, the university estimated that 620 students had left campus to join the army and the navy, and untold numbers of alumni had also joined the armed services, traveling to camps and bases all over the world. More ominously, by the time of the May 23 cap and gown convocation, fifteen former students had already been killed during the war, including two victims at Pearl Harbor, Ensigns Ira Weil Jeffery ('39) and Walter Willis ('39). Shouldn't someone be keeping track of the service records of students and alumni?

As it turned out, the alumni office was already on top of things. In fact, it had gone beyond simply compiling a list of the casualties of war and had begun a card file with approximately two thousand entries, detailing the service record of all the alumni it could locate. "Our sources of information are many and varied," Pierce wrote to Willey. "Deans' offices, newspapers, alumni themselves, and a special service set up by the American Alumni Council which gives us the camp location of Minnesota men at the time of entering service, but does not follow them through their changes." Notice of casualties was printed in the *Alumni Weekly*, as was an ever-expanding section on "Minnesotans in the Armed Forces."

THIS WAS ONLY THE START of a long labor. For the next three and a half years, the alumni office and the *Alumni Weekly* (which would soon become a monthly, published as the *Minnesota Alumnus*) were dedicated to the task of collecting and disseminating an ever-increasing mountain of information from and for its alumni members. From every corner of the globe came word of the men and women of the University of Minnesota who were serving the nation. And this information—sometimes sensitive, sometimes joyful, too often heartbreaking—was dutifully recorded by a newly created branch of the Alumni Records Office at the alumni association, the Alumni

War Records Office, and then published in the *Alumnus* to be sent out to readers of the magazine.

The collecting of stories of the whereabouts and well-being of thousands of Minnesotans in a world war was time-consuming and fraught with difficulties. Copies of each issue of the magazine were sent to the libraries and reading rooms of service camps and stations across the United States. Subscribers had their copies of the magazine delivered through armed services

Students in campus service training units (*Minnesota Alumnus, January 1944*)

Minnesotans in Uniform

Lt. Col. George W. Peterson '29A, has been named commanding officer at Rosecrans Field, training base of the ferrying division, air transport command, near St. Joseph, Missouri. Previously he was commanding officer at the ferrying division base at Brownsville, Texas.

Lt. Comm. Norman L. Mistachkin '31Md, is serving in the dispensary of the naval air technical training corps near Memphis, Tennessee. He has served in several places in the South Pacific. Present address: Co. N.A.T.T.C., Memphis 15, Tennessee.

Lt. (j.g.) Richard Carlson '33A; '34MA, is assigned to writing, producing and directing of training films for the navy. He is still under contract with Metro-Goldwyn-Mayer Pictures and will return to acting after the war.

Lt. John W. Harty '33E, has been in the South Pacific area for seven months. Before entering service in 1943, he was county engineer of Grand Forks county, North Dakota.

Lt. Kenneth D. Ruble '33Ex, former reporter and columnist on the Minneapolis Tribune and the Minneapolis Daily Times, is ordnance officer of his marine squadron overseas. His brother, Major Earl H. Ruble '33ChemE; '37MS, is in charge of

Lt Rudy Gmitro '41, Navy pilot and former Gopher halfback, was credited recently with assists in the sinking of two Japanese submarines near the Ryukyu Islands. He made the first bombing run over the submarines and other pilots followed to finish the job.

Lt. Clarence T. Johnson '38ChemE, of Hibbing, Minnesota, is ammunition chief with an infantry division of the First Army.

Lt. Philip Petersen '38Ex, of 3007 Humboldt Avenue North, Minneapolis, has been in service nearly four years. He served with the chemical warfare division in Africa, Sicily, and Italy. He now is in Southern France and recently had a reunion

The alumni magazine's "Minnesotans in Uniform" section helped readers track enlistments and where men had been stationed.

mail to wherever they were stationed. Each month, the magazine printed pleas for its readers to send information, and by early 1943, the magazine included a handy preprinted form that service people could clip and return to the Alumni War Records Office. This would provide the name, rank, University of Minnesota class, service address, and any additional information the writer might want to supply.

"Never before have so many Minnesota alumni moved so far, so fast and so often," reported the *Alumnus* in September 1943. "And never before have they written so many letters to the editor. This has helped us to keep track of their whereabouts and their activities but we need also the assistance of relatives and friends in completing our service records of alumni in uniform. The number of alumni in the armed forces or in related war work must now be near the 10,000 mark. . . . We are anxious to have news of assignments, training, promotions, awards and other information in these permanent University records." This was an increase of eight thousand servicemen and women in one year's time, and that number would continue to climb as the war progressed. Coverage of the doings of these graduates began to dominate the pages of the magazine. "Minnesotans in Uniform" featured notices of recent enlistments, stationings, and transfers. A column called "Letters from Here and There" contained missives from all over the world.

"Received the June *Minnesota Alumnus* here yesterday (August 5, 1943) which I always read with interest," wrote Colonel Abner Zehm (M.D. '28) from Sicily, where he was serving as a surgeon with an armored division. "After a brief Mediterranean cruise, I landed in the Gela section of Sicily on July 10, the day of our invasion of the island. I can assure you the cruise was not exactly a pleasure trip."

Lieutenant Ralph Britigan wrote from New Guinea in that same issue of the magazine: "I have enjoyed very much the issues of the *Alumni Weekly* and now the *Minnesota Alumnus* that I have received to date. . . . I enjoy the different photographs of the campus and the sections telling of alumni in service and in civilian life and their whereabouts and what they are doing. Would enjoy very much hearing from any Minnesota alumni situated in this part of the world."

There was chatty news in the February 1944 edition of the magazine about a joint gathering of University of Minnesota and Notre Dame alumni in London: "So pleasant was the occasion that it was suggested that the Minnesota and Notre Dame alumni get together again and there was a feeling that an ideal place for the next meeting would be Berlin." There were important clarifications made in the magazine as well. Florence Sacks, the wife of Lieutenant Marvin D. Sacks ('45), wrote in December 1944: "I noticed in your October issue of the *Minnesota Alumnus* a picture of my husband, and also the item saying that he was missing in the European area. I thought perhaps you might like to know that he has been reported a prisoner of war of Germany as of August 17, 1944."

The most heartrending news came in a monthly column, "Minnesota's Roll of Honor." Here were published the names of the war dead, as they arrived at the Alumni War Records Office. Each listing would typically give the name, class, rank, and branch of service of the victim; describe the action in which he was killed; and list a home address and the names of parents in Minnesota.

Occasionally, the magazine would offer more details. "With one brother killed in service and another a prisoner of war in Japan, Sgt. Robert H. Brain [class of '42], is being returned to the United States for permanent duty. . . . Sgt. Brain has been overseas 32 months and his latest assignment has been an air service unit in Rome. Lt. Stanley Brain [class of '40], Liberator bomber was killed January 16 [1945] at Harlingen, Texas. Cpl. Philip S. Brain (B.A.

'39), was taken prisoner at the fall of Bataan. For a time he was interned at Luzon, but since has been transferred to Tokyo." These were the sons of Philip Brain Sr., the university tennis coach and long a friend of the alumni association. Phil Brain had filmed Golden Gopher football games through the 1930s and put together the first highlight reels for viewing. These hugely popular movies were presented at alumni gatherings throughout the state.

The magazine used more photographs in its war issues than it ever had before. There were many service portraits: handsome men and women, smiling beneath their military caps, some caught forever young on the pages of the "Roll of Honor." There were 15 war dead listed at the alumni office in May 1942. By June 1944, that number had jumped to 193. In the last year of the war, the numbers rose dramatically. In December, the total was listed as 315. It was 520 in June 1945 and 568 in December 1945. Finally, 619 were listed in the February 1946 edition of the *Alumnus.*

In all, the Alumni War Records Office kept more than 12,000 individual records of Minnesotans serving in the armed forces during World War II.

News of Missing Pilot

It was a pleasure to receive the following letter with its message from Mrs. Marvin D. Sacks (Florence Klinsing), of Pipestone, Minnesota, whose husband, Lt. Marvin D. Sacks '45Ex, was reported as missing in action in the October issue of the ALUMNUS.

I noticed in your October issue of the MINNESOTA ALUMNUS a picture of my husband, and also the item saying that he was missing in

LT. MARVIN D. SACKS '45

the European area. I thought perhaps you might like to know that he has been reported a prisoner of war of Germany as of August 17, 1944.

Marvin was a co-pilot on a B-24 Liberator and went overseas in May, 1944. Their plane was shot down over Germany on July 12, 1944, while they were participating in their fifth mission over enemy territory. Through the Red Cross we heard that he was a prisoner. On October 5, 1944, he broadcast over short wave from Berlin from his prison camp. This, of course, was an enemy propaganda broadcast.

Marvin enjoyed his work at the University very much and perhaps after the war will return and finish his course. I want to thank you very much for the interest shown on your part in keeping track of as many former students as possible. May the war soon be over, so the young men and women may again return to their families, positions and schools, and to a normal American life.

Alumni followed news of soldier alumni and students, including the 619 who died in service during World War II.

Students and cars returned to campus following the end of World War II, 1946.

The magazine was sent all over the world, keeping homesick and weary University of Minnesota military personnel informed about each other and the doings on campus. For all its good work reporting the war as it was experienced by the university and its graduates, the *Minnesota Alumnus* won a national "Award of Excellence" from the American Alumni Council in 1944. "On behalf of my husband, Capt. Tobe S. Eberley (M.D. '42), who is in England with the Army air forces," wrote Marjorie Eberley to the magazine in June 1944, "I should like to tell you how much we appreciate reading the *Minnesota Alumnus*. I send each copy to him and he, together with several other Minnesotans, reads it from cover to cover. I'm sure the memories of happy days at Minnesota are greatly stimulated by your fine magazine."

As it turned out, the greatest service performed by the alumni association during the war was just letting university graduates know that the home fires were still burning.

School Spirit

Henry "Doc" Williams bandaging injured player during game, 1907
(photo by George E. Luxton)

The Upset

ON JANUARY 3, 1922, Colonel Eliel T. Lee, a thrice-wounded veteran of the Civil War and perhaps the biggest supporter of University of Minnesota football in the state, died in the Minnesota Soldiers' Home at the age of seventy-seven. He was buried a few days later in Lakewood Cemetery in Minneapolis. Known to a generation of Gopher fans as "The Man with the Flag," Lee had been a faithful attendee of all home football games for so many years that the exact count was lost. Until the very end, he brought an American flag to each game and waved it proudly on behalf of his team.

Adding charm to this tradition was the fact that Colonel Lee refused to let his flag fly over a Gopher defeat. In the fourth quarter of those games in which the home team was down by an insurmountable margin, Lee would quietly roll up his flag and slip out of Northrop Field before the final gun sounded. To thousands of fans, the sight of Lee packing up his staff and heading for the exit was a melancholy moment, a signal that the party was over.

Actually, the melancholy was pervasive with the University of Minnesota football program during the last two years of Lee's life. He and his flag had not witnessed the bitter end of many Gopher games through the 1920 and 1921 seasons. In fact, not since before Dr. Henry L. Williams first took the reins of the football program, twenty-two years earlier, had Minnesota football seen such miserable days.

Williams had long been considered one of the premier coaches in the nation. He was an innovator and "a strategist of the first water," according to Walter Eckersall, a widely read *Chicago Tribune* sportswriter of the era. Williams brought the newfangled and little-used forward pass to Minnesota in the 1910s, and his teams won or tied for conference championships in

1900, 1903, 1904, 1906, 1909, 1910, 1911, and 1915. In eight of his twenty-two years, the Gophers were undefeated; in eight more, they lost just one game.

Perhaps Williams's greatest team was one that didn't even win the conference championship. In 1916, the Gophers fielded a squad that outscored its opponents by the remarkable margin of 348–28, an average score of nearly 50–4. The only blemish in the schedule was an upset at Northrop Field, when Illinois came to town and stifled the vaunted Gopher passing attack.

The Gophers had decent records in 1917 and 1918, but World War I enlistments depleted the levels of football talent for programs around the nation, making the competition less than it had been in the past. Schedules also included service teams like the Chicago "Municipal Pier" squad—a group of all-star U.S. Navy recruits culled from various college football teams around the country—and a combined football squad of Carleton and St. Olaf players, which the Gophers thumped 59–6. The Gophers had another pretty good team in 1919, winning five of eight games, but two conference losses, to Iowa and Illinois, were galling and put Minnesota out of running for the Big Ten championship. For a football program accustomed to the successes that Minnesota had achieved through the first fifteen years of the century, a 5–3 record simply wasn't good enough.

Then came the disastrous 1920 season, during which the Gophers lost every one of their six conference contests. They rebounded to win two Big Ten games in 1921 but were crushed by Ohio State (27–0), the Wisconsin Badgers (35–0), the Iowa Hawkeyes (41–7), and the Michigan Wolverines (38–0). The once-proud Gopher football team was utterly humiliated, week after week sending Colonel Lee and his flag back to the Soldiers' Home with ample time for an early Saturday supper.

The consensus among Minnesota students, alumni, and fans everywhere was that something needed to be done—and quickly. It was easy to point the finger at the aging Coach Williams, with accusations that the game had passed him by, but as sportswriter Eckersall pointed out to Minnesota fans: To win games in a highly competitive conference like the Big Ten, a program had to do more than simply switch coaches. Top-quality athletes were needed and they had to be lured to the school by a variety of means. "Alumni of other institutions are constantly on the alert for promising athletic material," said Eckersall in a special analysis of the football program, written for the student paper *Ski-U-Mah*. "The grads have been instrumental in persuading boys to go far away to school, and when they arrived, positions of some kind were obtained whereby they could work their way through college."

The alumni association at the university agreed that something needed to be done, but its concerns went far beyond recruiting. At the end of the

1921 season, the alumni association formed a committee on athletics headed by former association president Henry Nachtrieb. These advisers met just days after the last game of the year and quickly counseled President Lotus Coffman and the Board of Regents via the pages of the *Alumni Weekly* "that the athletic system at the University is out of date." What was needed was a system established "along the lines followed at a number of other western universities." This meant creating a more professional athletic department headed by an athletic director "who shall give his entire time to that work." The committee also advised Coffman to fire all athletic coaches at the end of the year. This turned out to be the means by which the Gophers got rid of the man whose name had been inextricably linked to Minnesota football for more than twenty years.

Coffman, chairman of the alumni committee John Harrison, and regent Fred Snyder were designated as members of an interim athletic board. They asked for and received the resignation of all Gopher coaches and then

Football at the pre-stadium Northrop Field, which by the 1920s was unsuccessful at attracting top athletes proceeded to establish the university's first athletic department. To head this division they hired the university's first-ever director of athletics, Fred Luehring, previously of the University of Nebraska. A few days later, this same trio hired a new football coach, William H. Spaulding, who had been coaching football at Western Michigan University. The board then disbanded and turned over its work to Luehring, who proceeded to rehire the rest of the Gopher coaches, beginning with basketball coach Dr. Louis Cooke. Just one coach was not rehired: Dr. Henry Williams.

One other effort to boost the fortunes of the football program swung into full gear that winter of 1921–22, and it would turn out to be the biggest and most enduring change. The possibility of building a memorial stadium to honor the service of Minnesotans during the war had been discussed around the university since the end of World War I. Those talks, however, had never progressed into a constructive phase. That Northrop Field was small, old, and inadequate to the needs of a Big Ten football program was understood by all. But now, reinforced by the desultory performance of the Gopher squad over the past couple of years and the fact that a number of other regional schools had built mammoth stadiums, the need for a new playing field for the Gophers seemed clear.

Working in conjunction with the Board of Regents and a number of individual alumni, the alumni association helped form the Greater University Corporation, which became the fund-raising arm for Memorial Stadium. The stadium project was joined with efforts to build Northrop Auditorium, with the total price tag for the two buildings estimated at nearly $2 million. The funding campaign began in the fall of 1922 and was an immediate success. In less than a year, pledges from students, faculty, alumni, and other fans of University of Minnesota football had exceeded the $700,000 necessary to construct Memorial Stadium.

Ground was broken on the project in March 1924, and although it would take until 1929 to finish the fund-raising and complete construction on Northrop Auditorium, the bricks and mortar for the stadium were laid with amazing rapidity. On October 4, 1924, less than two years from the day the first dollar was donated, the Minnesota Gophers welcomed the University of North Dakota to their brand-new home and beat the Flickertails 14–0.

Coaching for Minnesota that day was William Spaulding, who had had a tough opening season for the Gophers in 1922, winning just two of six Big Ten games. Spaulding had experienced a promising second year at the helm, when for the first time in years Minnesota had actually vied for the Big Ten conference championship, beating Northwestern and Iowa and tying Wisconsin. But a loss in the season finale at Michigan ended any possibility of a 1923 title for the Gophers.

Unfortunately, that defeat turned out to be a portent of things to come in the 1924 season. After the North Dakota win, Minnesota lost twice and tied twice in its next four games, which meant that by mid-November the Gophers were winless in Big Ten play. Despite a fancy, new, fifty-thousand-seat stadium and a relatively new head coach, Minnesota had only a single victory, against the less-than-fierce Flickertails, to show for their struggles that season.

Memorial Stadium's bleachers under construction, 1924

It seemed as though the bad old days of Gopher football had returned. Adding to the sense of misery was the fact that the Big Ten season was scheduled to end on November 15 against the University of Illinois, which had what many considered the best football team in the country, headed by its star running back, the incomparable Red Grange. Only a junior at Illinois, Grange had already achieved legendary status, on a par with some of the other great sports figures of the 1920s, including Babe Ruth, Knute Rockne, and Jack Dempsey. In a game against powerhouse Michigan just a month earlier, on October 18, Grange had scored four touchdowns in under twelve minutes of play, a performance that was the talk of the football world all that fall. For the rest of the season, and in his senior year to come, fans poured by the tens of thousands into stadiums across the Big Ten to watch him play, and Grange would ultimately be named to three successive all-American teams at halfback. He was also christened with one of the greatest nicknames in sports history: the Galloping Ghost.

Aligned against the Ghost that upcoming Saturday were the Flickertail maulers, aka the Minnesota Gophers, who didn't look like they had a chance. All week long the local papers ran one profile after another of Grange, touting his skills, his modesty, and his accomplishments on the gridiron. There was not much ink left for the local boys. Adding to the gloom surrounding the game was the fact that university officials had decided weeks earlier to officially dedicate the stadium in this, the last home game of the season, against Big Ten rival Illinois. In other words, dignitaries and officials from around the state were about to gather with some fifty thousand other Gopher fans to bless the new sports facility and witness what one local sportswriter described as "Illinois in the role of the lion slay[ing] the lamb, portrayed by Minnesota."

The opening kickoff went to the Gophers, and they went no place fast. After three downs, Minnesota had gained seven yards and punted to Grange. Illinois proceeded to march down the field, and eight plays later the Galloping Ghost was sprinting into the end zone from the eleven-yard line. It was 7–0 Illini before latecomers had even warmed their seats.

But that eleven-yard touchdown by Grange would turn out to be his longest run of the day. Suddenly, every time he touched the ball, he was stuffed by a swarm of Minnesota tacklers. "Again and again 'Red' Grange hugged the ball to his ribs and started one of his famous runs," wrote Lorena Hickok in the next day's *Minneapolis Tribune.* "Again and again he started and dropped, with three or four Gophers on top of him."

Stepping forward on offense for Minnesota was its own halfback, Clarence Schutte, who, after a season of injury and undistinguished play, was himself doing a pretty fair imitation of the legendary Ghost. Schutte scored on Minnesota's first drive of the second quarter, and he scored again on the last drive of the half. He scored one more time in the third quarter, making the score 20–7 in favor of the Gophers. Late in that same period, Grange was gang-tackled one last time, so banged up by Minnesota linemen now that he had to be carried from the field. "On his shield, with injuries that may put him out for the rest of the season, we sent him back to Illinois Saturday night — 'Red' Grange the Incomparable, football's hero of heroes," wrote Hickok.

The final score was 20–7, in what was surely the most satisfying victory for a Gopher football team in years. Memorial Stadium had been well dedicated, and fair turnabout had been achieved for that 1916 upset of the University of Minnesota's undefeated team by Illinois.

It would be nice to report that the fortunes of the Minnesota football program rose on a steady course in the wake of the Illinois upset, but, in fact, the Gophers lost their very next, season-ending game to Vanderbilt, 16–0. What's more, Coach Spaulding would soon be replaced by Clarence Spears, and a couple more years of rebuilding loomed. By the 1930s, however, the University of Minnesota had established the best football program in the country under coach Bernie Bierman, continuing the great tradition that had been born in the days of Henry Williams. Minnesota won its first national championship in 1934 and would repeat that achievement in 1935 and 1936 and in 1941 and 1942. The team was undefeated in 1934, 1935, 1940, and 1941, and these last two teams featured the play of Minnesota's only Heisman Trophy winner, Bruce Smith.

The Gophers upset the Red Grange–led University of Illinois team during the last game of the season in the new 50,000-seat Memorial Stadium, 1924.

Henry L. Williams died in 1931, just a few years shy of the full-fledged return of championship Minnesota Gopher football. He apparently held no bitterness about his abrupt departure from the athletic department, and the university rewarded his continued support by honoring him with a banquet just four months after he was asked to leave his post.

Members of each of his teams gathered in the union ballroom for the occasion and presented Williams with a gold watch, a University of Minnesota blanket, and a silver football, which held the names of all the men who had received football letters under his coaching. The final gift was a U of M letter, stitched to a gold-colored sweater. All the old footballers choked back tears at this last presentation, according to the *Alumni Weekly*. "No man who has received an honorary L.L.D. from his alma mater," said Dr. Williams, "is half as proud as I am to receive this emblem of manhood from Minnesota."

In 1950, the university renamed its newly renovated basketball field house in his honor.

From Music Boxes to Meat

SINCE ITS FOUNDING IN 1904, the University of Minnesota Alumni Association has employed a variety of clever, novel, and—shall we say—interesting products to advertise itself, provide a service for its members, and make a few dollars for the association in the process. The Mug 'N Meat pack falls into the "interesting" category.

Mug 'N Meat was a line of university-crested coffee mugs handsomely packaged with two pounds of country sausage. In the late spring of 1963, the Mug 'N Meat distributor in Milwaukee contacted Ed Haislet, executive director of the Minnesota Alumni Association, wondering if the alumni association might be interested in selling these gifts to its members. The school's crest would be etched on the front of the mug in 22-karat gold, and the sausage would come in two varieties: summer (laced with spicy garlic) and hickory links ("especially perfect as party hors d'oeuvres with crackers or cheese").

The distributor's timing was perfect. His letter arrived just as Haislet was putting together the annual "Official University of Minnesota Gift Items" catalog, and the Mug 'N Meat pack sounded like it might be a nice addition. There was a problem, however. The distributor couldn't produce a University of Minnesota–crested coffee mug quickly enough to photograph it for inclusion in the gift item catalog, which was nearly on its way to press. What if, he suggested to Haislet, we shoot a Marquette University mug and do a little manipulation of the image? They would put a sharp focus on the "M," and the rest of the word—"ARQUETTE"—would be out of focus and disappear around the side of the mug. No one would know the difference, the distributor insisted. Catalog browsers would read the "M," and, where they saw only fuzz, their love of their alma mater would fill in "INNESOTA."

The MINNESOTA MUG 'N MEAT Pack

Haislet was obviously pressed for time, liked this Mug 'N Meat idea, and felt that the art might work. Who wouldn't want a slice of spicy summer sausage with a cup of Maxwell House on a Gopher football Saturday morning? He gave the go-ahead, and into the 1963–64 gift catalog went the Mug 'N Meat pack and its tantalizing description: "Make your coffee break a toast to your Alma Mater with this spanking white ceramic mug. . . . And for a companion snack, two lbs of all-beef smoked country sausages!"

It's hard to say whether the fallacies of the ad were detected by Gopher alumni and detracted from its appeal or if the time just wasn't right for the Mug 'N Meat concept. The bottom line, however, was that the package was not a hit. Haislet let his distributor down quickly and cleanly the following spring. "I know that you must have been disappointed in the number of Mug 'N Meat Packs sold," he wrote. "I was. I feel, therefore, that for the coming year we should drop the item."

The Mug 'N Meat pack had been just the latest in an explosion of what came to be called "loyalty items," marketed through the alumni association beginning in the 1950s. Whereas in the first half of the twentieth century, alumni association–affiliated products had been limited to a handful of publications, primarily university directories and references, gradually through the 1950s and 1960s an entire catalog of University of Minnesota souvenirs were marketed for alumni through the association — university blazers and blazer buttons, Minnesota playing cards and insignia serving trays, cigarette lighters and a musical cigarette box that played "The Minnesota Rouser" when you opened the lid and plucked your brand from within.

"Catalog" may be too grandiose a term for the marketing piece. The "Official University of Minnesota Gift Items" was a brochure whose presentation was a model of premodern salesmanship, featuring blunt copy with a hint of hard sell to it. "You Will Want Them," the text read, regarding the items inside. "*For Your Office *Your Home *For Your Own Use." "Perfect For: *A Birthday *An Anniversary *Graduation *Or Just a Gesture of Thoughtfulness."

An assortment of university-related gifts (Alumni News, March 1966)

The alumni magazine also served as a prime tool for selling loyalty items. The plum space on the back cover was typically reserved for advertising a rotating line of products. These included walnut chairs bearing the university logo silk-screened in gold on the seat back (priced at $27); university plates by Spode; and *Echoes from Memorial Stadium*, the first record ever cut of University of Minnesota songs.

Echoes was produced in 1953 and served as a kind of bridge project for the association between pre– and post–World War II alumni association sales efforts. Prior to the Ed Haislet era (1948–76), marketing of the association through product sales had meant producing and selling publications under the association's imprimatur. To E. B. Johnson, the first executive director of the association, this seemed a natural extension of the General Alumni Association's role.

Along with being a founding force in the association itself, Johnson had also created the alumni magazine, and he served as its editor through the first nineteen years of its existence. He was thus already inclined toward the publishing industry and encouraged the association to produce a string of books to help promote itself and spread the word about the university. All edited by Johnson himself, these books included some remarkably helpful reference tools: a *Dictionary of the University of Minnesota*, which was issued in two editions (in 1908 and with an updated version in 1911); a forty-year history of the university (1910); and several alumni directories.

Publishing, however, was an expensive and risky business to shoulder alone, and the university showed no interest in helping foot the bill for these early association efforts. By the mid-1910s, the association had decided it was wiser to contract with an outside publisher to produce its directories. The *Dictionary of the University* and any further alumni efforts at a general history also fell by the wayside.

In 1928, however, the alumni association was right back at it, publishing a history of the football program. Like the earlier references, this book was successful and remains a valuable historical tool; but as a stand-alone publication, it lacked the oomph necessary to perpetuate itself or other publications. Up until the 1950s, there were periodic calls to revise, update, and reissue a Gopher football history, but these efforts all came to nothing.

Meanwhile, the alumni association held what many considered a valuable asset, both in sentimental and marketable measures—the copyrights to a number of University of Minnesota songs, including "Hail! Minnesota" and "The Minnesota Rouser." Truman Rickard ('04), the composer of "Hail! Minnesota" as well as "The Ski-U-Mah Fight Song," had presented the rights for both these tunes to the association in 1926. The Minneapolis Tribune Company had held the rights to "The Minnesota Rouser," which accrued to it after sponsoring a fight song contest, won by Floyd Hutsell, in 1909. The Tribune Company presented the alumni association with the license to use this most popular of songs in 1928.

Exactly why the alumni association and not the university was given these rights remains a little foggy. At the time, distinctions between the university and the association were less defined than they would subsequently become.

A collection of songs to play and sing, offered by the alumni association, 1936

Apparently President Lotus Coffman felt the alumni association was a natural province within the university for all song-related matters. According to E. B. Pierce, the second executive director of the alumni association, "President Coffman preferred that the Association secure the copyrights, conduct competition for the new songs, and handle the whole song situation." And so it was.

Pierce subsequently signed a contract, on behalf of the association, with the Melrose Brothers Music Company of Chicago, giving that company publishing rights to the songs. It was easier and made more sense for the association to contract with a publisher than to go into the publishing business itself, according to Pierce. "A large music house has the staff and facilities for making arrangements and manifolding them as well as distributing them."

The album emerged during the dawn of a new era at the university and on college campuses across the United States. With the GI Bill, the university saw an explosion in its population. The growth in students meant a growth in graduates. The growth in graduates meant that the alumni association

A 12-inch long-playing record of concert, marching band, and glee club music, 1967

would be faced with many new members and many new opportunities. It was too early to say, in the late 1940s, looking out at the Quonset hut housing, the crowded classrooms, and the waves of students rolling over the campus, that someone was dreaming of selling all these future grads Mug 'N Meat packs. It is fair to state, however, that with this postwar tide of students a new and burgeoning market for university souvenirs and memorabilia was born. And the alumni association wanted to take advantage of it.

Enter Ed Haislet, who became the executive director of the association in 1948. Haislet was hired to help modernize the organization, which included finding new streams of revenue for its growing membership. One of Haislet's first suggestions was for the association to take advantage of

University President and Mrs. O. Meredith Wilson greet the class of 1912 at a reunion in 1962.

those association-owned university song rights and publish a songbook. This could be followed by a University of Minnesota LP record, and then another and another and another, all sold to the growing number of graduates pouring from the university.

The problem was that the Melrose Brothers Music Company was still around and still claimed the publishing rights to the university songs due to its 1928 contract signed by E. B. Pierce. A university lawyer was called in to look at the history of the rights, and he essentially determined that it was a mess and advised the alumni association to hire a New York law firm that specialized in copyright law to sort things out. There was a good deal of back-and-forth between law offices and the alumni association, but three years later, Ed Haislet was able to announce the outcome of the matter in a column in the *Minnesota Alumnus*, which he titled "Now We Can Sing." He might have added "finally": "Years ago the publishing rights to Minnesota songs was assigned to a commercial publishing house," wrote Haislet, "and because of ensuing copyright difficulties no record or album was officially published. In this day and age, when all the masters of the world of music are at our beck and call through high fidelity recordings the songs of the University of Minnesota have been conspicuously absent."

No longer. As of September 1953, *Echoes from Memorial Stadium*, featuring "Hail! Minnesota," "The Minnesota Rouser," "The Ski-U-Mah Fight Song," and other, lesser-known works such as "The Golden Gopher Line," was made available to alumni association members for the low price of $3.75, shipping included ($5 for nonmembers). The first order from the record company sold briskly. By May 1954, Haislet was asking for a second printing of five hundred LPs. Though sales slowed in subsequent years, until a second university album was recorded in 1963, *Echoes from Memorial Stadium* signaled the alumni association's entry into the brave new world of marketing memorabilia.

In years to come, the association kept expanding its souvenir offerings. In time, the "Official University of Minnesota Gift Items" catalog would include all of these items and more. There were pewter tankards and letter openers, plaques and paperweights, pen sets and glasses, end tables and bookends. There was a Gopher Helmet Radio and a Gopher Helmet Lamp ($14.95 each, in the 1976 catalog). The money didn't exactly pour in, but the gift items did bring in a steady line of income. The world of collectibles was enlarged and enriched, and the University of Minnesota Alumni Association had a good time improving it, including items like the popular "bobblehead" Goldy figurine and the practical insulated lunch bag.

As for the Mug 'N Meat pack? Perhaps Marquette University still sells it through an alumni catalog.

The Road to the Rose Bowl

I
N 1960, THE UNIVERSITY OF MINNESOTA was perhaps at the height of its prestige and renown. It was the largest university in the Big Ten and the fourth largest in the nation. Five United States senators — Hubert Humphrey (B.A. '39) and Eugene McCarthy (M.A. '39) of Minnesota, Wayne Morse (J.D. '28) of Oregon, Everett Dirksen of Illinois, and Quentin Burdick (J.D. '32) of North Dakota — had attended the University of Minnesota. The first open-heart surgery had been successfully performed at the University Hospital six years before, and its Medical School was known worldwide. But for sports fans, one measure of glory remained elusive: The Golden Gophers had yet to win the Rose Bowl.

In part, this was due to the simple obstinacy of the Big Ten. For years, conference members had jointly rejected post-season football bowl bids. The games were considered an excessive extension of a sport that already served as a distraction from the scholarly pursuits of student athletes and ordinary students alike. This sensibility changed in the post–World War II era, and by 1949, the Big Ten was eager to join in the New Year's Day football fest and agreed that a conference representative would accept an invitation, if offered, for the next Rose Bowl in Pasadena, California.

In January 1949, the executive board of the Minnesota Alumni Association revealed a pretty sunny outlook on the possibility of future bowl bids by naming a committee "to determine the percentage of the total tickets which should be made available for alumni, to determine the criteria for selection of alumni to receive tickets, and . . . the method for handling tickets requested on the basis of the criteria determined." It would be eleven years before any of these matters became of practical importance, and even then, at the start of the 1960 football season, few would have predicted that the Golden Gophers would be making the cross-country trip come January.

The team had won just two games the season before, and the Big Ten, especially Iowa, was loaded with talent. For the Gophers, quarterback Sandy Stephens had played well on occasion as a sophomore, and there was a quality line, including Tom Hall. But as the gun sounded on the close of a season-ending win over Wisconsin, fans could be forgiven for their surprise. The 8–1 Gophers were the new Big Ten champions.

The 1961 Rose Bowl program from the Gophers' first trip to Pasadena

Earlier in 1960, however, the Big Five (the forerunner to today's Pac-10 conference) had decided to offer its 1961 Rose Bowl bid to the number one team in the nation instead of the Big Ten champion, as had been its custom for the previous dozen years. No matter. A couple weeks after the end of its regular season, the Big Ten champion Gophers were the number one team in the nation. Students spilled into the Minneapolis streets when word came that the team was ranked number one in both major football polls and had finally received an invitation from Pasadena. For the first time in University of Minnesota history, the Golden Gophers were headed to the Rose Bowl.

But for executive director Ed Haislet (B.S. '31) and the alumni association, it was no simple chore to organize for the event. When the invitation finally came and the planning wheels started spinning, they immediately became stuck in the mire of ticket distribution.

Rose Bowl sponsors were notoriously tight about doling out tickets to their Big Ten guests, and Gopher fans experienced no exception to this tradition. A Tournament of Roses Committee appointed by recently named university president O. Meredith Wilson created a priority list based on the past experiences of Big Ten schools visiting the Rose Bowl. The list began with what was deemed "the official party"—including the team, coaches, university administrators, and the governor. Then came a class of university benefactors, "civic and state leaders," and alumni who had donated more than $100 to the university. Beyond these were students and faculty, dues-paying alumni association members, and season-ticket holders. The fact that some benefactors and civic leaders got their tickets before many of the alumni association members meant that Haislet would spend months afterward opening letters from irate Gopher fans grousing about the unavailability of tickets.

Haislet had smaller matters to deal with as well. Another alumni correspondent, signed "An Ardent Gopher Fan," had some advice that he or she wanted passed on to the cheerleading squad regarding their costumes for the Rose Bowl: "Because the white shorts used by the cheerleaders simply emphasize bulging fannies and look more like underwear than anything else—PLEASE get the girls back into skirts and the men into regular trousers for the Rose Bowl game. I am proud of our team and I want to be proud of our cheerleaders, too. All season they looked ridiculous in their B.V.D.'s. Please have a bon-fire of these track shorts and get back to skirts and trousers for the Rose Bowl."

Most moods had improved by the time a group of special alumni association–sponsored, Rose Bowl–bound trains left Minneapolis on December 26 for a ten-day trip to the West Coast. The tour included a five-hour layover in Las Vegas, daylong trips to Disneyland and Knott's Berry Farm, tickets to the Tournament of Roses Parade and the Rose Bowl Game, and accommodations at the swank Biltmore Hotel. An added twelve-day "exclusive jet tour" to Hawaii, after the game, was optional. On New Year's Eve day, the *Minneapolis Tribune* reported that the plush Beverly Hills Hilton hotel had hosted a gala for the visiting entourage from Minnesota the evening before. Stars at the party included emcee Bob Hope, as well as Zsa Zsa Gabor, Gene Autry, and Gordon MacRae. Photos captured Gopher players in cheek-to-cheek grins with young blonde starlets.

Whether heads were turned by all this glitterati is hard to judge, but the fact of the matter is the team came out flat on game day, January 2, 1961. The Gophers played the first half in a California smog of their own making and fell behind their opponents, the Washington Huskies, by a score of 17–0. Their second-half play was more representative of the team that had ended the season number one in the nation, but, sadly, the Gophers couldn't overcome the deficit and lost 17–7.

It was an era when the West Coast–Midwest sectional rivalry was intense. Newspapers from San Diego to Seattle felt little compunction about kicking the Gophers when they were down. "Watching Minnesota clomp ponderously about the grass last Monday, you had trouble envisioning this group as the top-ranked team in America," wrote one Los Angeles columnist. "Some of their backers insisted lamely that the Gophers at the start merely got left in their holes, but it's an immutable fact that even when they got to running they didn't show enough speed to catch a porcupine."

For once, however, the phrase "there's always next year" held true. In the fall of 1961, the football team returned Sandy Stephens and all-American Bobby Bell. The Gophers played well during the season but finished in second place in Big Ten conference play. However, because of a faculty council dispute, champion Ohio State turned down an invitation from the Rose Bowl committee, and the University of Minnesota football team found itself, once again, on the road to Pasadena.

And, once again, Ed Haislet was beset by ticket requests. About 6,500 West Coast alumni contacted the alumni association offices wanting a good chunk of the fewer than 17,000 tickets allotted to the Big Ten representative. Not all of them could be accommodated. There were also complaints about the fact that two-thirds of Minnesota ticket holders were placed in the end zone—another indignity imposed upon all visiting Big Ten teams by Rose Bowl organizers.

The Biltmore Hotel was once more used as home base for alumni association boosters, but instead of taking the train to the West Coast, charter alumni groups flew—a first for Big Ten alumni groups visiting the game. A trip to Disneyland remained a part of the tour package. The pregame party

All-American linebacker–defensive end Bobby Bell played on both Gopher Rose Bowl teams.

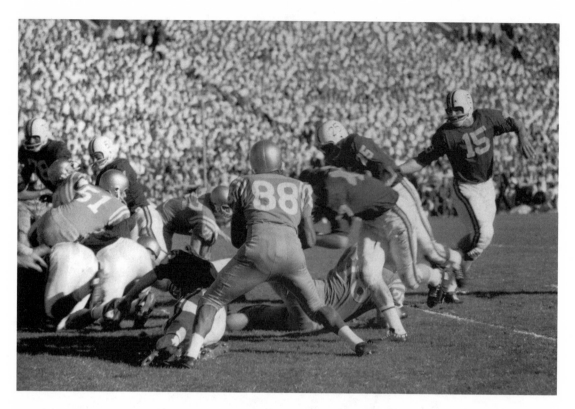

was again headlined by Bob Hope, but Minnesota's own Halsey Hall was brought in to serve as toastmaster and, according to Haislet, "ran the best party ever." The Golden Gopher hospitality room at the Biltmore featured free Hamm's beer and cheese from the American Dairy Association of Minnesota. Regarding the refreshments, Haislet noted in a subsequent column in the *Alumni News* that "peculiar as it may seem, less beer was consumed this year than a year ago—but almost double the amount of cheese was used."

Maybe the more pronounced midwestern flavor to pregame festivities made the Gophers more comfortable this time around. Or maybe it was just their due. But unlike in their first Rose Bowl, the Golden Gophers played a superb first half against their opponents, the UCLA Bruins. With touchdowns from Stephens and Bill Munsey, Minnesota took a 14–3 lead into the locker room and never looked back. The final score was 21–3, and at the end of the game the Gophers hoisted Coach Murray Warmath on their shoulders and strode off the field into the Pacific sunset.

Up in the press box, West Coast reporters typed their stories with far less glee than they had a year earlier. Any gloating that could be heard in the Pasadena night came from alumni in the cheap seats in the end zone, and it felt pretty hard-earned.

A rose to any other coach could never smell so sweet as did this bloom to Murray Warmath returning to Minnesota with the winners of
Rosebowl 1962

Coach Murray Warmath receiving a rose on his return to Minnesota after winning the 1962 Rose Bowl

Watching the Minnesota-Michigan football game enacted on a large blackboard, about 1925

Notes on Sources

Guns and Scholars

James Gray, *The University of Minnesota, 1851–1951* (Minneapolis: University of Minnesota Press, 1951); Elmer A. Adams, *Recollections of Early Minnesota Days* (Fergus Falls, Minn., 1949; and E. Bird Johnson, ed., *Forty Years of the University of Minnesota* (Minneapolis: General Alumni Association, 1910), were all helpful in giving background information on the early history of the university. Laurence Vesey, *The Emergence of the American University* (Chicago: University of Chicago Press, 1965), provided valuable insight into the changing nature of higher education in the 1880s.

The *Ariel* (also known as *The Ariel*) was published in twenty-three volumes, from December 1877 to April 1900. The first student-edited journal to be published at the University of Minnesota, the *Ariel* provided a number of editorial comments on the incident, as noted in the story. Local newspapers and the *New York Times* were also fascinated by the events of May 1882 at the university.

The Broom Brigade

The *Ariel* was rife with talk of "Company Q" through the fall of 1888 and into the spring of 1889. The Gratia Countryman quotes come from a reminiscence she wrote of Company Q that can be found at the University of Minnesota Archives in the Gratia Countryman Papers, 1866–1953, "Letter to Mrs. Siegelman, re: Company Q, 1951." Also helpful was a history of the School of Kinesiology at the Web site of the College of Education and Human Development at the University of Minnesota: http://education .umn.edu/KLS/school/history.htm. A story by Gretchen Kreuter, "Equal Time," *Minnesota*, November/December 1987, also provided good background.

Trailblazers and Jim Crow

Aside from Adams's *Recollections*, Andrew Hilyer's years in Minneapolis were documented through periodic references in the *Ariel*, which continued to track his career after Hilyer moved to Washington, D.C.

The St. Paul newspaper the *Appeal*, which can be found in the newspaper archives at the Minnesota Historical Society, was the most diligent chronicler of African American students at the University of Minnesota. A 1905 article in the *Appeal* listed the first seven black graduates of the university. According to the paper, they were Hilyer; Frank Wheaton (the first African American graduate of the College of Law, 1894); McCants Stewart (College of Law, 1901);

Scottie Primus Davis (the first African American woman graduate, 1904); William Ricks (College of Law, 1905); and two brothers, Walter B. Holmes and Eugene P. Holmes, who were the first students of African American descent to graduate from the Colleges of Medicine (Walter in 1894) and Dentistry (Eugene in 1893). Evidence suggests that the two brothers, who were of mixed-race ancestry, lived their lives apart from the African American community in Minnesota.

An index to African American newspaper articles found at the Minnesota Historical Society, compiled by Brendan Henehan, was an invaluable tool in finding individual citations to the lives of African American students at the university. The incident at the Oak Tree Restaurant was found in this way. Similarly, Bobby Marshall's athletic career can be tracked through the index and local newspaper coverage. The Ku Klux Klan incident was front-page news on January 13 and 14, 1923. The incident involving William Morrow occurred in April 1921 and was reported in the *Minnesota Daily*. The university annual, the *Gopher*, provided some limited reference to early students and topics such as the student days of Roy Wilkins.

Interviews conducted by the author with Mark Soderstrom, Barbara Cyrus, and David Taylor in November 2001 were invaluable to the story. Soderstrom provided a working paper, "'A Segregated House Is a Hitler House': Students, Workers, Educators, and the Battle for Desegregation at the University of Minnesota," which provided background for the article. "The Negro File, 1921–1936," in Box 22, President's Office Papers, at the University of Minnesota Archives added the correspondence about nursing school applicants and housing issues. Stories in the *Minneapolis Spokesman*, cataloged and partially indexed at the Minnesota Historical Society, covered both the dorm and *Porgy and Bess* controversies, as did the *Minnesota Daily* (October–November 1939).

A Place for Women

Background on the life of Ada Comstock at the University of Minnesota comes from Barbara Miller Solomon, *From Western Prairies to Eastern Commons: A Life in Education, Ada Louise Comstock Notestein, 1876–1973*, edited by Susan Ware; and Roberta Yerkes Blanshard, "Ada Louise Comstock, Some of Her Memories of Her Life up to 1843, Collected for Reading to the Saturday Morning Club, March 16, 1974." Sections of the book and the recollections (which contain the Comstock quotations), as well as a few copies of the *Shevlin Record*, were found at the University of Minnesota Archives.

The Great Flu Epidemic and Ruth Boynton's Health Service

The *Minneapolis Tribune*, the *Minnesota Daily*, and the *Minnesota Alumni Weekly* from the months of September, October, November, and December 1918 provided information on local responses to the influenza pandemic of that year and coverage of the widening crisis. Statistics on the number of cases seen by the newly created University Health Service were published in *The President's Report, 1918–1919*. John Sundwall's address, "The Inauguration of the Health Service Program at the University of Minnesota," which was delivered at the dedication of the first health service building (not the Boynton Clinic), served as a history of the early years of the student health service at the university. It can be found in the Students' Health Services Papers, 1918–1943, at the University of Minnesota Archives. These papers provided background on Ruth Boynton's tenure at the student health service. In addition, the archives maintain a small collection of Boynton's own papers (Ruth Evelyn Boynton Papers, 1931–1962), which likewise provided background on her life at the university. Also helpful were the Presidents' Annual Reports, which continued to provide statistics on visits and concerns to the health service clinics.

Background on the pandemic of 1918 comes from John M. Barry, *The Great Influenza: The Epic Story of the Deadliest Plague in History* (New York: Viking, 2004); and Gina Kolata, *Flu: The Story of the Great Influenza Pandemic of 1918 and the Search for the Virus That Caused It* (New York: Touchstone, 1999).

General Custer and the Geology Professor

Sources for General Custer include Herbert Krause and Gary Olson, *Prelude to Glory* (Sioux Falls, S.D.: Brevet Press, 1974); Donald Jackson, *Custer's Gold* (New Haven, Conn.: Yale University Press, 1966); Evan Connell, *Son of the Morning Star* (San Francisco: North Point Press, 1984); and the Newton H. Winchell and Family Papers at the Minnesota Historical Society. (See also Newton Horace Winchell Papers, 1872–1908, at the University of Minnesota Archives.) See Newton H. Winchell, *Geological Report on the Black Hills* (Washington, D.C.: Government Printing Office, 1875), for specific details on his work in the Black Hills. For stories on the fate of Custer's dog, Cardigan, see the *Minneapolis Tribune*, March 21–27, 1923.

"A Spectacular Career"

Brendan Henehan, the creator of the index to African American newspapers at the Minnesota Historical Society, is probably the leading authority on the life of J. Frank Wheaton. The author's interview with Henehan in April 2004 was extremely helpful in creating this profile. A brief biography of Wheaton exists in Marion D. Shutter and J. S. McClain, ed., *Progressive Men of Minnesota* (Minneapolis: Minneapolis Journal, 1897). In addition to the newspaper articles referenced in the story, the *Ariel* noted Wheaton's studies as a law student at the university, and the *Appeal* carried a number of stories about him during his years in Minneapolis. When Wheaton moved to New York, his exploits were still occasionally covered by Twin Cities African American newspapers, and stories of his work in Harlem were included in the leading African American newspaper of the era in New York, the *New York World*—though its Republican editorial slant was often at odds with Wheaton's Democratic politics. Coverage of Wheaton's death and funeral can be found in the *World* and the *New York Times*.

Remembering Roy Wilkins

Roy Wilkins, with Tom Mathews, *Standing Fast: The Autobiography of Roy Wilkins* (New York: Viking Press, 1982), is the best source for Wilkins's childhood and life in St. Paul and at the University of Minnesota. Gilbert Jonas, *Freedom's Sword: The NAACP and the Struggle against Racism in America, 1909–1969* (New York: Routledge, 2005), provided insight into Wilkins's thoughts on other civil rights movement leaders. Newspaper articles on Wilkins's later career and his periodic visits to the university are collected in a Roy Wilkins Folder at the University of Minnesota Archives.

Behind Gate 27

Details on the life of Ancel Keys come from an interview by the author with Dr. Keys in November 2000; from Ancel Keys, *Adventures of a Medical Scientist: Sixty Years of Research in Thirteen Countries* (Ancel Keys, 1999); and from an interview with Dr. Henry Blackburn, also in November 2000. Blackburn's biography of Keys at www.epi.umn.edu/keys was also consulted. The University of Minnesota Archives provided the resources and expertise in tracking the development of the Division of Epidemiology from its roots in Physical Education through the Laboratory of Physiological Hygiene. The March 16, 1937, "Letter to Diehl" and the "Letter to Coffman from Diehl, April 27, 1937" are from the Office of the President Records, Collection

841, File: Medical School, Lab of Phy. Hygiene, Dept. of Phy Ed. 1937–39. The Ancel Keys Papers are now at the University of Minnesota Archives.

King Red

Joseph Blotner's biography, *Robert Penn Warren* (New York: Random House, 1997), provided background for this article, but most of the references to Penn's life in Minnesota came from the Robert Penn Warren Folder at the University of Minnesota Archives.

Farsighted Foresters

Newton Searle, "Minnesota National Forest: The Politics of Compromise, 1898–1908," *Minnesota History* (Fall 1971), is the best single source on the creation of the Chippewa National Forest. Issues of the *Courant*, the journal of the Minnesota Federation of Women's Clubs, which can be found at the Minnesota Historical Society, provide most of the color in this article. The forest controversy was a preoccupation of the Women's Clubs beginning in 1899 through the creation of the forest.

For more on Maria Sanford, see Barbara Stuhler and Gretchen Kreuter, ed., *Women of Minnesota: Selected Biographical Essays* (St. Paul: Minnesota Historical Society Press, 1998). The University of Minnesota Archives also has a collection of Sanford's papers.

Sex and the Psychology Professor

The Harlow Stearns Gale Papers, 1889, 1939, are at the University of Minnesota Archives. Within that collection is Robert T. Laudon, *The Gales of Music* (Minneapolis: The Author, 1997), which is a history of the Gale family's influence on the music community in Minneapolis by a professor emeritus in the Music Department at the university. This book provided background on Gale

and his family. So did David Kuna, *The Psychology of Advertising* (Ph.D. diss., University of Minnesota, 1975), also found in the Gale Collection at the archives. Gale's own writings, in particular *Ideals and Practices in a University: A Pedagogical Experiment* (Minneapolis: Vineyard Press, 1904), were the source for Gale's confrontations and dealings with Cyrus Northrop. This book and other writings by Gale can be found, along with his correspondence, in the Gale Collection at the archives.

The Fight for Academic Freedom

William B. Riley and his role in the debate on evolution are thoroughly covered in Ferenc M. Szasz, "William B. Riley and the Fight against the Teaching of Evolution in Minnesota," *Minnesota History* (Spring 1969). C. Allyn Russell, "William Bell Riley: Architect of Fundamentalism," *Minnesota History* (Spring 1972), was also helpful for background on Riley. Articles in the *Minnesota Daily* and the *Minnesota Alumni Weekly* in February and March 1927 highlighted the importance of the debate as it was happening. Included among these stories is Lotus Coffman's address to the Senate Education Committee in the March 10, 1927, *Minnesota Daily*.

No Other Moment Like This One

Interviews conducted by the author in November 2002 with Bill McMoore, Clarence Taylor, David Taylor, Matt Stark, John Wright, and Gloria Williams provided the basis for this story. The Office of the Dean of Students, Records, 1904–1968, at the University of Minnesota Archives provided much useful information on post–World War II race relations on campus, particularly Box 11 (for surveys detailing racial problems); Boxes 12 and 23 (for Panel of Americas information); and Boxes 29 and 37 (for information on African American student organizations, the Afro-American Action Committee, and Students for Racial Progress). Also helpful were the Student Activities Bureau Records, 1911–1977.

The Ph.D. and the Northeastern Fisheries

Quotations were taken from Elliott's diaries, Charles B. Elliott Papers, in the library at the Minnesota Historical Society. In June 1937, *Minnesota History* published extracts from those diaries, which included many of the same entries that the author used here. That article was edited for publication by Charles B. Elliott's son, Major Charles W. Elliott. Providing general background for the story was Thomas Bailey, *A Diplomatic History of the American People* (Englewood, N.J.: Prentice Hall, 1980).

Iron Mike

Information on Theo Alice Ruggles-Kitson and her work comes from John D. Meakin and Susan I. Sherwood, "Profiles in Corrosion," September 1998. This is the final report of a joint University of Delaware–National Park Service research effort to evaluate the role of environmental factors in the corrosion of outdoor bronze sculptures. A copy of the report can be found in a biographical folder, "Theo Alice Ruggles-Kitson," at the University of Minnesota Archives. The early coverage of the Spanish-American War and the fate of University of Minnesota students in the Philippines appeared in a series of articles in the *Ariel*, running from the late spring of 1898 into the following year.

To Hudson Bay and Beyond

Eric Sevareid, *Canoeing with the Cree* (St. Paul: Borealis Books, 2005), provided the bulk of the source material for this story. Also consulted were Sevareid's memoir, *Not So Wild a Dream* (New York: Atheneum, 1976); and Raymond A.

Schroth, *The American Journey of Eric Sevareid* (South Royalton, Vt.: Steerforth Press, 1995).

Beneath Saudi Sands

Much of the information on Fred Davies's years at Aramco comes from the William E. Mulligan Papers (Box 1, Folder 10), which are collected at Georgetown University in Washington, D.C. Mulligan was an employee of Aramco who worked in that company's public relations department. Brief articles on Davies can be found in *Minnesota*, March 1947, and *Alumni News*, March 1975. Davies's role in the discovery of Saudi oil is also told in Wallace Stegner's history of Aramco, *Discovery: The Search for Arabian Oil* (Beirut, Lebanon: Aramco, 1971).

"What Is Our War Job?"

The *Minnesota Alumni Weekly* became a monthly magazine and was renamed the *Minnesota Alumnus* in 1943. Issues of both magazines provided much of the content for this story. Also providing background on the gathering of information on university students involved in the war effort were the Papers of President W. C. Coffey and the Papers of the Alumni Association (particularly Box 16), both at the University of Minnesota Archives.

The Upset

Colonel Eliel T. Lee's obituary can be found in the January 12, 1922, edition of the *Minnesota Alumni Weekly*. The *Weekly* provided much of the background for this story, including details on changes in the football program and athletic department (see issues from December 1921 and January 1922, in particular). The General Alumni Association of the University of Minnesota also published a history of university football in 1928 (Martin Newell, ed., *The History of Minnesota Football* [Minneapolis: General Alumni

Association, 1928]), which offered a detailed view of the program under Coach Henry Williams.

The best stories on the game itself came from the *Minneapolis Tribune*. Those interested will note that the reporter for the *Tribune*, Lorena Hickok, went on to greater fame in the1930s and 1940s as the close friend and confidante of Eleanor Roosevelt.

From Music Boxes to Meat

The early gift catalogs of the University of Minnesota Alumni Association can be found in the Alumni Association Papers at the University of Minnesota Archives. Also found there is the correspondence of Edwin Haislet, which provided information on vendors. The complicated issue of who holds the copyrights to university songs is the subject of a great deal of correspondence, which is also found at the archives in a few different locations, including the President's Office Record, 1911–1945 (in a folder marked "Copyright"), and under the file "Songs of the University." *Minnesota, Hats Off to Thee*, a history of the university band, 1892–1992, published by the University of Minnesota Band Alumni Society, in 1992, has an interesting historical section, "Songs of the University of Minnesota."

The Road to the Rose Bowl

The Minnesota Alumni Association Records, 1881–1990, at the University of Minnesota Archives were essential to telling this story, particularly Box 14, which contains alumni association plans for both Rose Bowl trips, correspondence with alumni about the events, and clippings about the games and pre- and postgame happenings.

Photograph sources

The photos on pages 126 and 130 are courtesy Mark Luinenburg; on pages 158 and 161, courtesy the Special Collections Department, J. Willard Marriott Library, University of Utah.

The photos on pages 4, 7, 10, 11, 14, 15, 17, 20, 21, 22, 26, 29, 34, 35, 37, 40, 41, 43, 44, 46, 48, 64, 73, 76, 79, 81, 83, 84, 86, 91, 92, 93, 106, 120, 123, 125, 128, 134, 135, 153, 179, 182, 183, 186, 187, 190, 193, 194, and 195 are courtesy the University of Minnesota Archives. All the other images are from the Minnesota Historical Society collections.